# WORKING CHILDREN IN
# NINETEENTH-CENTURY LANCASHIRE

# Working Children

# in

# Nineteenth-Century Lancashire

*edited by*
*Michael Winstanley*

Lancashire County Books 1995

*Working Children in Nineteenth-Century Lancashire*
Edited by Michael Winstanley

Published by Lancashire County Books, 143 Corporation St., Preston,
in association with the Lancaster Branch of the Historical Association.

**British Library Cataloguing-in-Publication Data**
A CIP catalogue record for this book is available from the British Library

ISBN 1-871236-40-1

Lancashire County Books is part of Lancashire County Library Service and has as its remit the
publication of books and pamphlets with academic and general appeal dealing with all aspects of
the history of the county.

The Historical Association (founded 1906) is a national organisation with branches throughout
the country. It provides a range of activities and publications at national and local level for people
who share an interest in, and love for, the past. Further details can be obtained from Historical
Association, 59a, Kennington Park Road, London SE11 4JH.

The two organisations have collaborated to further these aims and to produce a series of high
quality, illustrated pamphlets and short booklets written by acknowledged experts in their fields,
designed to bring some of the fruits of recent scholarship to a wide audience.

Already published in this series:
John K. Walton, *Wonderlands by the Waves: a History of the Seaside Resorts of Lancashire* (1992).
Jeffrey Richards, *Stars in Our Eyes: Lancashire Stars of Stage, Screen and Radio* (1994).
Robert Poole, *The Lancashire Wakes Holidays* (1994).

Typeset by Carnegie Publishing, 18 Maynard Street, Preston
Printed in the UK by Redwood Books, Trowbridge, Wilts.

# Contents

# Tables and charts

## Tables

## Charts

# Abbreviations and notes

*Abbreviations used in references:*

PP        Parliamentary Papers (encompassing official bills, statistical returns, enquiries by Select Committees and Royal Commissions). These are available for consultation on microfiche at Lancaster University Library.

LRO     Lancashire County Record Office, Bow Lane, Preston.

ibid.     the same work as the previous reference.

*Currency conversion:*

12*d.* (twelve pence) = 1*s.* (one shilling) = 5p.
20*s.* = £1

# *Acknowledgements*

I WOULD like to thank everyone who has helped to make this book possible. First and foremost are the students who participated so enthusiastically in the project. I know that for some it turned out to be much more of a commitment (some might even say ordeal) than they anticipated, but I hope that they will think that the effort has been worthwhile. Education is, or should be, a two-way process and I have learned much from working with them. Many others have contributed significantly along the way including the staff of Lancaster University Library, Lancaster City Library, and Lancashire Record Office; Elizabeth Roberts who allowed us access to the Centre for North West Regional Studies oral history archive which she had collected; my colleagues Dr Stephen Constantine and Dr John Walton for invaluable support and comments on drafts; Jim Pressley for his knowledge of the half-time system; and last, but not least, Zoë Lawson of Lancashire County Books, who initially had the idea for a book on this subject and who has had the confidence to back the idea of writing it as a collaborative venture from the start. My thanks to you all.

Michael Winstanley
Lancaster University
December 1994

# The book and its contributors

Most of the original research for this book was carried out by twelve undergraduates in the History department at Lancaster University over two academic terms in 1993–4. They had registered for a course which was advertised as a 'group research project' dealing with the subject of child labour in nineteenth-century Lancashire. Their tutor told them that he expected them to write a book. Gradually it dawned on them that he was not joking; but it was only when he produced a contract that they *really* knew he was serious. We hope that you enjoy what we have produced.

Four of the chapters were researched and written by pairs of students working together. The exceptions are chapters 1 and 2. The first chapter originally contained descriptions of children's jobs during the industrial revolution which Leslie Willis had collected; this material has been merged with two studies of various aspects of the cotton industry and original material collected by the editor to produce a totally new chapter 2. I have then added some general thoughts to Malcolm Fielding's detailed, original analysis of the census. Wherever possible, the accuracy of the information in all the other chapters has been checked. Occasionally I have included additional illustrative material which I discovered during the editorial process when I thought it appropriate to do so, and I have sought throughout to make links between the chapters and to produce a uniform written style, but essentially the structures of the chapters, the material and the interpretations are those of the students who researched them.

In writing the book we have sought to appeal to anyone with a general interest in the past but we also hope that we have made an original contribution to historical knowledge. The book has only been able to include a fraction of the information which we collected and there is still plenty of scope for further research on this rich and fascinating subject, some of which, no doubt, will qualify our conclusions. Consequently we have included detailed references to sources which we have consulted and I have listed some ideas for further study, in the hope that some readers will have sufficient interest to pursue the subject further. This includes an annotated, select bibliography of some of the excellent studies of children and childhood which historians have produced in recent years, and a brief guide to sources which are relatively accessible in local archives and libraries.

Chapter 1

# Lancashire children in the nineteenth century

*Malcolm Fielding and Michael Winstanley*

VICTORIAN Lancashire, like the rest of Britain, resembled a Third World country of today in one important respect – a large proportion of the population was young. In 1851, the date of the first census to collect reasonably accurate figures on the population's ages, some 46 per cent of the two million people in Lancashire were aged under twenty, with even higher concentrations outside the largest cities of Manchester and Liverpool. In excess of one in three were under fifteen.[1] Those under twenty still comprised nearly 40 per cent of the county's population in 1911, while three out of every ten people were under fifteen.[2]

It should come as no surprise to find, therefore, that what the young did, or did not do, and the conditions under which they grew up, attracted widespread concern throughout the period. Childhood and work were not viewed as incompatible by many contemporaries, but the extent and nature of that work were central to discussions about children's and adolescents' intellectual, physical, moral and spiritual welfare. From a national perspective, Lancashire had a high concentration of factory labour. As the centre of the industrial revolution, with a higher than average proportion of children at work, Lancashire remained prominent in debates on child labour although, as we shall see, cotton did not dominate the entire county and there were considerable changes in the type of work which children did which also generated expressions of concern.

## *Themes and sources*

Subsequent chapters in this book describe and explain some of the day-to-day realities of the varied work which children in the region undertook in the century before 1914 and the attitudes of adult society towards it. In this opening chapter we will introduce briefly several general themes which underlie the issues explored in later chapters. However, we will concentrate first on assessing and explaining Lancashire's distinctive experiences. We will look at the volume and nature of children's work throughout the county, consider how it differed between towns and between boys and girls, and explore how patterns changed over time.

We need to remember that the events discussed here all took place against the backdrop of arguably one of the most dramatic periods of flux in British society in recorded history – the progressive development of the world's first industrialised society. These changes were accompanied by the emergence of new ideas and values which included a redefinition of the concept of 'childhood' itself, in both the age range which it was thought to encompass, and the activities which were seen as acceptable, or desirable, during it. For most of the period attention was focused on those up to fourteen years of age and this book naturally follows this definition. However, it also includes material on the life of those in their teens who were not yet absorbed into adult society. These juveniles or 'young persons', as they were referred to during most of the century, attracted increasing attention from the 1890s. The later chapters reflect this growing concern.

To gain as full a picture as possible, the historian of child labour needs to consult a variety of sources. Broadly speaking there are two types of sources: statistical data, collected by government and interested individuals and organisations; and contemporary commentaries, including official enquiries, the work of social reformers and published or oral first hand accounts. We need to bear in mind at the outset that the unpaid work which many children did was in the home and is largely absent from official statistical records, as is much of the informal, part-time paid employment which they often undertook. The sources also reflect changing social concerns and should not be taken as exact representations of

Boys doing exercises to music, Whitefield School, Nelson, *c*. 1912. By the 1900s elementary education had expanded its narrow curriculum which emphasised training in basics to reflect growing concern about the physical welfare of children. (Lancashire County Library, Nelson Library Local Studies Collection)

reality, but taken together and handled carefully they can yield valuable information and insights.

Prior to the mid-nineteenth century, we have to rely virtually exclusively on patchy and localised sources: newspapers, letters, diaries, published itineraries and tracts, or official government enquiries into specific industries, notably textiles. Detailed examinations of the social and economic condition of Britain became more common from the 1830s and were especially prominent in Lancashire where the Manchester Statistical Society, the first such group nationally, was founded in 1833 to collect information on a wide range of issues.[3] Such publications and enquiries, while informative so far as they go, were selective and do not provide a comprehensive view of all aspects of society. The first national census was taken in 1801, but it was only from 1841 that information was collected on individuals' ages and occupations, although even then ages were approximate since most individuals were returned under five-yearly age bands. By

3

1851 detailed abstracts of the data were produced which allowed a picture of the entire nation to be compiled. From then on the decennial censuses provide us with an extremely useful, and increasingly informative, quantitative estimate of numerous aspects of society, including children's work. The enormous amount of time and energy devoted by the Victorians to this exercise in itself informs us of a developing social self awareness – a curiosity to know about society and its operations, and the causes and thus the potential remedies of its ills. Comparisons over time still need to be made cautiously, however, since the areas covered, the definitions employed and the categories used all changed, while the concerns of the period themselves could, and did, influence the collection and presentation of the evidence. Nevertheless it is possible to make meaningful comparisons between the figures in different censuses on child employment. For this reason, much of this opening chapter relies on this particular source and concentrates on the period from the mid-nineteenth century to the end of the Edwardian period: we have selected four censuses, those of 1851, 1871, 1901 and 1911, to provide a basis for the analysis.[4]

## *How different was Lancashire?*

What, then, do we know about children's work, the age at which it commenced and how it changed over time? Historians disagree both about the extent of child labour before the mid-nineteenth century and whether it was increasing or decreasing.[5] It is widely believed that 'throughout the eighteenth century, children were regularly employed from the ages of five or six',[6] but it is likely that, for much of their early upbringing, children were more of an economic liability than an asset, since they were unable to undertake sufficient remunerative work to provide the income necessary to support them. Most of the jobs which very young children did were irregular, unpaid, and usually part of family-based workgroup, often in the home or an adjacent workshop. This was the case both in agriculture, where certain jobs like harvesting involved the whole community, and in industries like textiles and some metal trades which were largely carried out in domestic workshops. Even in occupations outside the home, like mining, children often worked alongside relatives. Young children, especially those under ten, rarely, if ever, worked independently and were not trusted, or able, to undertake skilled or heavy manual labour. It is quite likely, given the rapid expansion in population from the late eighteenth century, that jobs for children, boys and girls alike, became increasingly difficult to find in some parts of the country.

The first national survey of occupations was the census of 1841. Although the national government carried out only limited analysis of such information, the original enumerators' manuscript books have survived, and these allow us to explore details for specific areas and to build up local pictures of what children did. For example, 10–14 year olds in the township of Skerton (just to the north of Lancaster) are listed as performing a variety of jobs and display the three major characteristics of their paid employment which remain evident throughout the century. First, more boys than girls were listed as being in work: 65 to 54. Secondly, textiles provided the largest number of jobs for both boys (28) and girls (40): silk, cotton and woollen mill workers; woolcombers and sorter; spinners, weavers and a twinespinner. Thirdly, there was a greater diversity of work for boys. The only other occupation listed for girls was 'servant' (14). Seven boys were also servants, but there was also a long list of other job opportunities open to them: apprentices (10); joiners or carpenters (3); tailors (3); agricultural workers (2); general labourers (2); masons (2); a coach-maker; carter; cooper; sawyer; shoe-maker; stay-maker; painter, wright and white smith.

From 1851, the increasing details in the published census enable a much fuller picture of children's work to be obtained. The first observation we can make is that they seem to confirm the view that few children below the age of ten were regarded as being 'in work'. Nationally only just 36,000 out of the 2 million children aged 5–9 were recorded in occupations: 2 per cent of boys and 1.4 per cent of girls. Lancashire's figures were above the national average, but only just, at 2.8 per cent for boys and 1.6 per cent for girls. The highest county percentages were not in the North but in Buckinghamshire, Hertfordshire and, in particular, Bedfordshire where 11.9 per cent of boys and 21.4 per cent of girls were recorded as working. The common characteristic of these counties was the survival of the domestic industries of lace-making and straw plaiting which were organised on the putting-out system, with the work undertaken for the most part in the home or small workshops. Lace schools were regarded as one of the most notorious exploiters of young children – the schooling was more or less cursory, the work hours often extremely long and the conditions (damp and poorly lit rooms) damaging to health.[7] Nationally straw plait work and lace-making accounted for over a third of all very young girls' employment, but agriculture was the largest single employer of boys in this age group.

In Lancashire, however, it was textiles, and in particular cotton, which provided most work for boys and girls below ten, with only coalmining recording any other significant number of boys. The census does not break down these categories further but, since family-based domestic handloom-weaving is known to have survived into this period across much of central and north-east Lancashire, it is likely that some of these young children were employed in this and not in factories.[8] Local census-based studies of handloom-weaving townships like Mellor, near Blackburn, suggest that very young children were listed as being employed in this domestic trade.[9] But nationally the absolute numbers of such children were small and, as a result, after 1871, the 5–9 year-old category was excluded from the census tables on children's work – there were not enough working to make it significant.

Far more children aged 10–14 worked in 1851, some 352,600 boys and 189,000 girls nationally, representing 36.6 per cent and 19.9 per cent of the age group respectively. Lancashire, again, had figures above the national average, well above in the case of girls. However, its rates were not the highest in the country. The woollen and worsted industries of the West Riding relied heavily on child labour, and higher percentages of boys were also employed in those counties which still had significant pockets of textiles, leather work, metal trades and pottery which were either carried out in or around the home, or in small scale businesses, and in the mining districts of Cornwall. The domestic industries of lace-making and straw plait work continued to provide much employment for girls in South Midland counties.

Extract from a census enumerator's book for Oswaldtwistle, 1851. Although only one head of household on the schedule worked in cotton, the industry dominated employment patterns for children and juveniles. (Lancashire County Library, Accrington Local Studies Collection)

*Table 1.1*
*Counties with higher percentages than Lancashire of 10–14 year-old children
returned as occupied in the 1851 census*

| Boys | | Girls | |
|---|---|---|---|
| W. Riding of Yorkshire | 51.6 | Bedfordshire | 50.6 |
| Bedfordshire | 49.6 | W. Riding of Yorkshire | 35.9 |
| Northamptonshire | 47.6 | Nottinghamshire | 35.1 |
| Cornwall | 46.7 | Buckinghamshire | 34.0 |
| Staffordshire | 46.5 | Derbyshire | 33.8 |
| Warwickshire | 44.8 | | |
| Buckinghamshire | 44.0 | | |
| | | | |
| Lancashire | 43.7 | Lancashire | 33.7 |
| England and Wales | 36.6 | England and Wales | 19.9 |

These percentages, however, disguise the fact that the sheer size of the populations in the textile and associated industries of Lancashire and the West Riding of Yorkshire dominated national employment figures. Lancashire alone accounted for 15.8 per cent of all working children (13.7 per cent of boys, 19.7 per cent of girls) aged 10–14 in England and Wales, while the West Riding had a further 12 per cent. No other county approached the numbers found in these areas. The proportion of children employed also fell more dramatically in other counties like Staffordshire and Warwickshire over the next two decades than it did in Lancashire, and this meant that the county's relative importance in the child labour market increased still further. By 1871 15.9 per cent of all 10–14 year-old boys and 22 per cent of girls recorded as being in work in England and Wales were in Lancashire.

## Differences within Lancashire

Statistics relating to the county as a whole, however, conceal very considerable diversity of places and lifestyles, and Lancashire's percentage figure was depressed by the fact that large tracts of the county were not dominated by textiles. In terms of its area, if not its population, Lancashire was still largely rural, and areas such as the Fylde and Furness continued to have a distinctive, primarily agricultural identity. Small market towns, such as Poulton-le-Fylde, Garstang and Ulverston remained largely un-touched by the industrial revolution except for isolated factories in the early years of the century, taking advantage of both the relatively cheap labour and the availability of water power. But many larger towns in the county also had very different employment patterns which offered fewer opportunities for children's work. Unfortunately, the published census statistics in 1851 on individual towns, as opposed to counties, only provide a breakdown of employment for 'principal towns' under two very broad age groups: those under twenty and those twenty and over. Despite the fact that considerable numbers of infants and of young adults were therefore included in the figures, we can nevertheless get a good idea of the difference between towns from Table 1.2.

*Table 1.2*
*Percentage of under 20s in work in principal Lancashire boroughs, 1851*

|  | Boys | Girls |
|---|---|---|
| Oldham | 37.4 | 30.9 |
| Blackburn | 35.9 | 32.4 |
| Preston | 33.8 | 31.8 |
| Bolton | 33.5 | 28.4 |
| Manchester & Salford | 30.5 | 25.8 |
| Lancaster | 27.5 | 25.1 |
| Liverpool | 23.8 | 14.9 |

Source: *Census of Great Britain 1851, Division VIII (North West), Occupations of Males and Females under 20 and 20 and upwards in Principal Towns.*

The figures recorded for textile towns like Oldham, Blackburn, Preston and Bolton were among the highest in the country; only the worsted towns of the West Riding, the silk town of Macclesfield and the cotton-based economy of Stockport recorded higher percentages for both girls and boys. In view of the low numbers of under-tens in work, figures in excess of 35 per cent probably represent near full employment for older children and teenagers. Also noticeable is the high level of female employment in the textile towns, which approaches that for males.

9

It was the low figures for children working in the large commercial centres, particularly Liverpool, and to a lesser degree Manchester, which depressed the average figure for the county. These cities had more in common with London and other commercial and maritime cities elsewhere in the country than they did with the textile areas of Lancashire. Manchester had much lower levels of industrial employment than the neighbouring textile towns of Bolton or Oldham, and much more in the way of casual jobs like running messages for boys and domestic service for girls, emphasising that it was not simply a cotton town writ large, but a commercial and trading centre with a very different social structure.[10] The contrast between Liverpool and the industrial towns is even more dramatic. Here there was little in the way of regular work for either boys or girls, and none of the concern expressed over the employment of children in cotton factories: just the reverse. It was the *lack* of jobs for children which exercised the minds of the local authorities. Giving evidence to the government's Children's Employment Commission, Sir Joshua Walmsley, mayor of the city in 1839–40, expressed concern that unemployed children were being left by their parents to run wild in the streets and were turning to crime. He considered that

> the great fault in Liverpool was a want of employment for children; there were hundreds who had been brought to live by plunder; they herded together in cellars 20 or more in a place without a bed to lie on, and sallied forth from these dens at all hours to pilfer and steal what they could find.

These sentiments were echoed by the Reverend Mr Carter, chaplain of the borough prison, who commented that 'there was a great want of employment for children in Liverpool and though many got an education in consequence of this, there were many children of poor parents who, by not being profitably employed, ran wild and became regular thieves and pilferers.'[11]

It would wrong, therefore, to equate Lancashire solely with cotton in the mid-nineteenth century; it was a varied county and generalisations about what children within its boundaries did in the way of work conceal great diversity, in terms both of the jobs available and the experiences of childhood generally. This variety is a central theme of the chapters in the rest of this book.

## Changes in children's work: 1851–1911

The census, then, provides a valuable insight into the distinctiveness of Lancashire's experience in mid-century, as well as a reminder of the differences that existed within the county. It is also the most comprehensive source for understanding subsequent changes. Although the 5–9 year-olds cease to be recorded separately after 1871, the census provides increasingly detailed information on the work of 10–14 and 15–19 year-olds, and in 1911 it included a breakdown of occupations in all the county boroughs by age group, allowing the picture to be brought into even sharper focus. Although there was increasing concern expressed about the nature of adolescent employment by the 1900s, we will continue to concentrate on 10–14 year-olds in this chapter to facilitate comparisons with earlier periods.

Arguably the most important trend in child labour is revealed in Table 1.3 which shows the percentages of this age group which were returned as being in work in 1851, 1871, 1901 and 1911.

*Table 1.3*
*Percentages of 10–14 year-olds recorded as working*

*Lancashire*

|  | *1851* | *1871* | *1901* | *1911* |
| --- | --- | --- | --- | --- |
| Boys | 43.7 | 41.5 | 28.5 | 25.6 |
| Girls | 33.7 | 28.2 | 21.4 | 19.9 |

*England and Wales*

|  | *1851* | *1871* | *1901* | *1911* |
| --- | --- | --- | --- | --- |
| Boys | 36.6 | 32.1 | 21.9 | 18.3 |
| Girls | 19.9 | 20.5 | 12.0 | 10.4 |

Source: *Census of Great Britain, 1851–1911.*

What we see here throughout the period are falls in the percentages of children working in both Lancashire and the country at large which are particularly noticeable after 1871. The county's figures, however, remained substantially above the national ones, especially for girls, and the

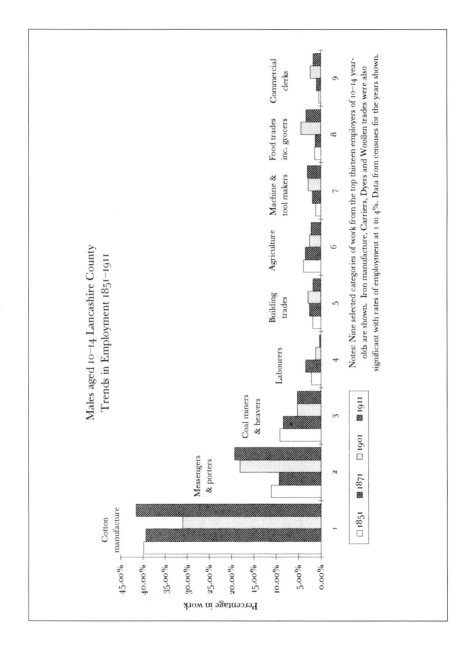

Males aged 10–14 Lancashire County
Trends in Employment 1851–1911

Notes: Nine selected categories of work from the top thirteen employers of 10–14 year-olds are shown. Iron manufacture, Carriers, Dyers and Woollen trades were also significant with rates of employment at 1 to 4%. Data from censuses for the years shown.

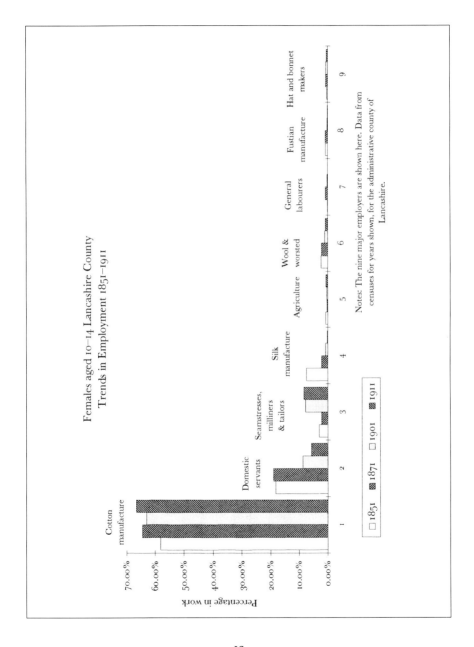

Females aged 10–14 Lancashire County Trends in Employment 1851–1911

Notes: The nine major employers are shown here. Data from censuses for years shown, for the administrative county of Lancashire.

differential widened rather than narrowed over the period as numbers of children in employment elsewhere in the country fell at a faster rate than they did in Lancashire. By the end of the century, in other words, Lancashire's experience had become more distinctive than it had been fifty years earlier.

Charts 1.1 and 1.2 give some indication of the structure of children's work in the county over the same period. What is immediately apparent is that there was a continuing difference in the nature of job opportunities open to boys and girls. The range of paid work available for girls remained very restricted: cotton, domestic service, and tailoring trades accounted for 86 per cent of female work in this age group in 1851 and 79 per cent in 1911. A similar pattern existed for females aged 15–19. Cotton alone accounted for over 60 per cent of girls' employment throughout the period, and actually increased in importance as wool, silk and, less dramatically, fustian manufacturing in the county declined. Domestic service was much less significant than it was elsewhere in the country and both the numbers employed in it and its relative importance fell, in contrast with those in clothing-related work: seamstresses, milliners and tailors.

By contrast, boys were employed in an expanding range of trades. Cotton remained the major employer but there was a substantial increase in service-related employment: messengers, porters, errand and shop boys, commercial clerks. Considerable growth also took place in machine- and tool-making and, at least until 1901, building trades. These replaced earlier dependence on coal-mining, agriculture and general labouring. After the age of fifteen the range of jobs available for boys expanded still further, with cotton taking a less central role – those who remained in the industry tended to aspire to higher status, skilled and supervisory posts in spinning, in contrast to the girls and women who dominated weaving.[12]

If we look at individual towns a remarkable diversity is again evident. The exceptionally detailed material in the census of 1911 however, itself a symptom of an increased concern about children's and adolescents' labour at the time, allows us to explore this phenomenon in more depth than for 1851.

Although fourteen was now the official school-leaving age, it was possible to work part-time in many districts by obtaining partial exemption at the age of twelve and full-time exemption at thirteen by reaching a

A group of mill workers at Burnley. Most youngsters engaged in manual work adopted both the headgear and the stance of the adult employees. (Lancashire County Library, Burnley Local Studies Collection)

specified educational standard or making a minimum number of attendances in a year. Despite this, in much of Lancashire in 1911 few children were recorded as being in work before the age of thirteen: only 1 per cent of 10–12 year-olds were in employment in Manchester and Liverpool. However, the figures were much higher in the cotton districts, especially the weaving areas of north-east Lancashire: over 40 per cent of 12 year-old boys were employed in the county boroughs of Blackburn and Burnley, and over 60 per cent in Bacup, Great Harwood, Darwen, Crompton and Oswaldtwistle. The proportion of 12 year-old girls working was even higher than that for boys in Blackburn, Great Harwood, Clayton-le-Moors, Walton-le-Dale, Preston, Bury, Clitheroe and Church. By the age of thirteen the figures were much higher in all these places, rising to well over 80 per cent in most of the weaving districts. Even outside the textile areas it was not unusual for a substantial minority of boys aged thirteen to be in work, although in Barrow, Blackpool, Bootle, Liverpool and Southport the figure was below 5 per cent and in Manchester it only touched 13 per cent. Girls' employment patterns were similar. Figures were very high in the weaving districts, with over 80 per cent of 13 year-olds employed in Bacup, Great Harwood, Crompton, Oswaldtwistle, Church and Darwen, but elsewhere they were generally much lower than boys'.

*Table 1.4*
*Percentages of 14 year-old girls and boys recorded as in employment*
*Lancashire Towns 1911*

| Girls | | Boys | |
|---|---|---|---|
| Burnley | 87.2 | Oldham | 90.7 |
| Rochdale | 85.3 | Blackburn | 90.2 |
| Oldham | 84.3 | Burnley | 89.3 |
| Blackburn | 84.1 | Bury | 89.2 |
| Bolton | 83.4 | Bolton | 87.1 |
| Bury | 81.0 | Wigan | 86.0 |
| Preston | 78.4 | Preston | 85.8 |
| Wigan | 70.8 | Rochdale | 85.3 |
| Salford | 61.3 | Salford | 78.8 |
| Manchester | 58.0 | Warrington | 77.9 |
| Rural Districts | 56.8 | St Helens | 77.8 |
| Warrington | 54.9 | Manchester | 74.1 |
| Southport | 34.1 | Rural Districts | 71.5 |
| Liverpool | 27.3 | Barrow | 69.9 |
| Blackpool | 27.1 | Liverpool | 53.7 |
| Barrow | 23.5 | Blackpool | 52.9 |
| Bootle | 20.9 | Southport | 52.7 |
| St Helens | 18.6 | Bootle | 52.2 |
| | | | |
| Lancashire (total) | 58.0 | | 74.9 |

Source: *Census of Great Britain* (1911), Lancashire Table 23.

Table 1.4 shows the percentage of children employed on finally leaving school at the age of fourteen. Paid work for children in some areas was still clearly in short supply. The textile towns continued to offer most opportunities for both boys and girls, while Liverpool and Bootle provided little in the way of regular work for either. The situation, therefore, was much the same as in the 1840s when Walmsley expressed his fears. Boys found plenty of work in the heavy industrial and mining towns, but girls had few opportunities in these towns, especially St Helens and Barrow. The low figures for the seaside resorts are possibly misleading, since, as we shall see, many children were engaged in family guest houses and businesses and are unlikely to have been recorded.

## Explaining the changes

Clearly, children's experiences of work continued to be very much influenced by the nature of the local economies in the areas in which they grew up. Only the cotton industry offered approximately equal opportunities for boys and girls. Elsewhere in Lancashire girls had far less chance of obtaining paid employment than boys and the jobs they did were very different. This largely reflected contemporary views about what was considered fit and proper work for girls to do. A decline in the proportion of 10–14 year-olds recorded as being in work is common to both boys and girls, however, and a number of explanations have been put forward to account for this.

The increasing volume of legislation controlling or outlawing certain kinds of child labour is often considered to be a major cause of this decline. Controls over work in textile factories and mines in the early nineteenth century (see chapters 2 and 3), were gradually extended to cover other sectors of the economy. In particular, Acts of 1864, 1867 and 1878 controlled children's labour in workshops, and the Employment of Children Act in 1903 restricted involvement in street trading. In addition, the age at which a child could legally work in industry was progressively raised. The Factory Act of 1874 raised the minimum age of employment to ten to take effect from 1876. In 1893 the minimum age was raised to eleven and in 1899 it was increased again to twelve (from 1900). Such legislation reflected changing attitudes towards children in society. Originally there had been an expectation that young children, at least those of the lower classes, would work; Walmsley's complaint about Liverpool in the 1840s was that there was insufficient work to keep children away from bad influences, not that there was too much work being done by children to the detriment of their education. Concerns which had initially been expressed only about severe and excessively harsh conditions, however, gave way in the latter

Scholars from Ripley Orphanage, Lancaster, dressed up for the opening of the new town hall in January 1910. The orphanage, established in 1864, catered for children from the Lancaster and Liverpool districts. Its existence reflected the fact that a significant proportion of young children lost one or both of their parents while they were still young. (Lancaster City Council, Museums Service)

half of the nineteenth century to a different view of childhood which emphasised its distinctiveness from adulthood and the disadvantages to the individuals concerned, and to society at large, of allowing children to work from too early an age. Childhood was becoming synonymous with school.

The introduction of the principle of compulsory education and the gradual extension of the period during which children had to be at school was also responsible for the decline of child labour. Prior to the 1870s the only children who were required to attend school were those who worked in trades covered by the Factory and Workshop Acts, and pauper children in workhouses. The Education Act of 1870 sought to ensure that there was adequate educational provision throughout the country and subsequent legislation gradually increased the powers of local authorities to extend the period during which children were compelled to attend school and to lay down the conditions under which they would be allowed to work, part- or full-time, before they reached the age of fourteen. The Elementary Education Act of 1876 stipulated that children between and ten and thirteen could be employed only if they had attained certain standards of proficiency in reading, writing and arithmetic, or had achieved a specified number of attendances. Thereafter, many local authorities gradually increased the minimum standard or number of attendances which had to be achieved before a child could begin work.

Some historians have suggested that these restrictions were not the main cause of the decline in numbers working as parents were voluntarily taking the initiative to remove their children from the labour market to ensure that their offspring obtained a sound education. They point to the steady rise in living standards in the last quarter of the century which gave parents the option of being able to keep children at school, instead of needing to send them out to work at an early age. This has also been linked to the growing strength of trade unions which sought to prevent employers undercutting adult wages by employing juveniles and children.

Yet, as we have seen, there were considerable differences in the patterns of children's work which cannot be accounted for purely by legislation or increasing prosperity. Indeed, children's work persisted in textiles which had been the first industry to be subject to legislative controls. Trade unions in cotton Lancashire continued to express considerable support for the view that *some* work for children was beneficial and necessary, and parents, employers and unions continued to exert pressure on local authorities to allow children to leave school early or to obtain partial exemption (chapter 3). Far from being the poorest areas of the county, the textile districts were also those most closely associated with increasing affluence, which enabled institutions like the Co-op to take hold early and promoted the growth of commercial leisure activities like professional football, the music hall and the seaside holiday. The high wages which adult male spinners earned may have encouraged some of them to keep their children, especially the girls, at home, but in the weaving areas, especially those districts which specialised in coarse cloth and which were already beginning to feel the effects of foreign competition, and where adult wages were comparatively low, it was the ability of children to earn from an early age which contributed to the modest prosperity which many families enjoyed. In the casual labour markets of cities like Manchester and especially Liverpool, where standards of living were much lower and trade unionism much weaker, many working-class parents did not have the option of sending their children out to work early because there was no regular work for them to do.

Legislation, education and parental attitudes, therefore, can provide only a partial explanation of the patterns of child labour. This is because they ignore the demand for young workers. If, as would appear to have been the case up to the early nineteenth century, children's employment in manufacturing had generally been undertaken as part of family units often working on piece rates, sometimes in a domestic setting, then the demise of much of this form of production would undoubtedly have affected the numbers employed. Industry, in other words, offered less and less scope for child employment as the century progressed. This was the case in mining and virtually every manufacturing industry including lace-making, shoe manufacture, pottery and nail-making, all of which, as we have seen, had accounted for high levels of children's employment in some counties up to the 1850s. Evidence collected in Lancashire for the Children's Employment Commission as early as the 1840s clearly showed that, apart from the cotton industry, children under fourteen were largely engaged in trades like nail-making and hat manufacture which were still carried out in sheds attached to domestic cottages. There were fewer employed in trades which were not based in or around the home: iron foundries, machine-making, glass manufacture, bleaching and dye works, and paper-making. Technology was also beginning to undermine much of the work which they undertook. Young children employed in turning the spindle in rope-making, for example, were steadily being replaced by machinery. Springs fitted to doors were eliminating the need for door-tenders in mines, and where larger seams in pits allowed for installation of tramways and the introduction of larger waggons, juveniles and young adults were required to haul coal from the pit face to the surface.

Why, then, did child labour survive so long in cotton, the industry which exhibited the first and most dramatic transformation of production? The answer lies partly in the nature of the work, and partly in the strong familial and communal networks which existed in the textile towns. Although the technological innovations from the second quarter of the century rapidly destroyed the domestic household economy in which children had previously participated, the organisation and nature of work in the factory still depended heavily on small groups of workers being responsible for a limited number of machines, whether they were carding machines, spinning mules or power looms. All of these required regular attention to function properly. As in domestic industry, adults were paid on piece rates; that is, what they earned was determined by how much they produced. In these circumstances, adult workers were effectively working for themselves, and they found it profitable to employ children as cheap assistants since they helped to increase productivity. Supervision of children, therefore, was not the responsibility of the manufacturer, but the worker, and it was facilitated by the extensive family networks and close-knit communities in the textile towns which ensured that children were subject to a variety of controls from adults both in and outside work.[13]

## Part-time and family labour

Although the census can be used to shed considerable light on the patterns of child employment during the period, it would be wrong to place complete reliance upon it. Much of the work in which children were engaged was casual, part-time or seasonal and, then as now, often remained unrecorded in official documents, observed only by those intimately involved with it. Many continued to work not for employers but for their families and they were rarely paid on their own account. As we will see, even if we discount the undoubted importance of the unpaid housework and child-minding which girls performed in the home, the extent of this work was quite considerable.

While it was true that regular, waged employment was less available outside the textile districts, this did not mean that young children elsewhere in the county did not work at all. They were often employed without pay wherever small-scale, family businesses remained the norm, notably in farming, retailing, services, and the provision of accommodation, the last becoming especially important in the expanding seaside resorts from the 1870s. Girls were also expected to help at home with housework and the rearing of younger brothers and sisters. Labour-intensive commercial and retailing services and transport activities also provided increasing part-time work for boys towards the close of the century, many of which, despite their different titles – shop boy, messenger, porter, van boy, telegraph boy – essentially amounted to the running of errands. Such jobs were particularly common in the cities, especially Liverpool, where they were also virtually the only openings available on leaving school.

Unlike employment in the cotton factories, which required regular hours and was strictly controlled by law, most of these other jobs which children did were unregulated and could generally be combined with full-time schooling, since this only occupied six to seven hours per day for less than two-thirds of the year. Some worked before and after school; others were employed on Saturdays; yet others were kept away from school, with or without permission, during busy times of the year. Education authorities invariably made allowances to accommodate this, by scheduling extended school holidays for busy times of the farming year, for example, or by enabling children to take extended leave of absence during the summer in seaside resorts if they attained a minimum number of attendances or reached a specified standard of educational proficiency.

Compulsory schooling, therefore, restricted the opportunities for full-time employment, but it did not prevent children from undertaking some work. The half-time system, as it was widely known, allowed children to alternate factory work and school on a daily basis while many others worked in non-school hours. Both types of work were coming under increasing criticism by the 1900s but neither was banned. The half-time system remained in place until 1918 while the Inter-Departmental Committee on the Employment of School Children, which reported in 1902, proposed specific controls on activities like street trading, but concluded that a 'moderate' amount of labour was beneficial, rather than detrimental, to children's development, especially if it was supervised by members of their families. It was widely accepted that education had abolished most of the evils associated with idleness or certain forms of child labour. By the 1900s concern had largely shifted to what 'young persons' did, or did not do, once they left school. Many simply continued to do full-time what they had previously done part-time. As the census figures show, mill work in the textile districts absorbed the bulk of school-leavers, but elsewhere in the county the labour market did not provide sufficient full-time employment, and that which it did provide, at least for boys, was increasingly considered to be unsuitable since it offered no industrial training or discipline.

## Conclusion

Cotton clearly dominated children's employment in much of Lancashire, therefore, but there were other forms of work, part- and full-time, which did not feature in the census returns and which have been largely neglected by historians of the county. The following chapters, therefore, emphasise the diversity of childhood experience in Lancashire. Chapter 4 deals with Lancashire's distinctive pattern of farming; chapter 5 explores the range of service employments open to boys, especially in the commercial cities of Manchester and Liverpool, and chapter 6 discusses the opportunities open to girls outside the textile districts. It is cotton, however, and the early industrial revolution, which still dictate popular conceptions of the county and rightly so, since the industry dominated the economy of many Lancashire towns. Above all, it was cotton which generated the first debates about child labour which led to a series of legislative interventions by government designed to control the conditions of children's work. It is with cotton, therefore, that we begin our survey.

## References

1. Manchester and Liverpool had 41–43% of the population aged under 20, with higher proportions found in boroughs such as Blackburn (49%) and the rural district of the Fylde (47%).
2. By way of contrast, in 1991 only about 30% of the British population were under 20 and only just over one in five under 15.
3. See T. S. Ashton, *Economic and Social Investigations in Manchester, 1833–1933* (London, P. S. King, 1934; repr. Brighton, Harvester, 1977).
4. Out of a very large number of listed employments, the thirty most significant numerically have been selected and followed over the four censuses. In practice the top dozen or so most common jobs (shown in the charts for 10-14 year-olds) accounted

for the vast majority (80% or more), of children recorded as occupied in Lancashire for most of the period and for all three age groups, 5–9, 10–14 and 15–19.

5.  H. Cunningham, 'The Employment and Unemployment of Children in England, *c.* 1680–1851', *Past and Present*, 126 (1990), pp. 115–50 provides an excellent review of the debates and the sources on which it is based.

6.  N. Tranter, 'The Labour Supply, 1780–1860', in R. Floud and D. McCloskey (eds.), *The Economic History of Britain since 1700*, 2 vols. (Cambridge University Press, 1981), i, p. 221. Similar views can be found in many textbooks.

7.  Further information on children in the lace industry is to be found in W. B. Stephens, *Education, Literacy and Society* (Manchester University Press, 1987).

8.  G. Timmins, *The Last Shift: the Decline of Handloom Weaving in Nineteenth-Century Lancashire* (Manchester University Press, 1993), pp. 107–24.

9.  I. Holland, 'A Study of the Township of Mellor as a Handloom Weaving Settlement using the Census Enumerators' Books' (unpublished M.A. dissertation, University of Lancaster, 1993), p. 60.

10.  A. Kidd, *Manchester* (Ryburn/Keele University Press, 1993), p. 25.

11.  *Children's Employment Commission*, Report of A. Austin on Trades and Manufacturing in Lancashire, PP, 1843, xv, p. M69.

12.  The data on which the above comments are based is taken from the tables of categories of employment by age for Lancashire, in the four censuses, 1851, 1871, 1901 and 1911. Abstracts were prepared for this investigation.

13.  P. Bolin-Hart, *Work, Family and the State: Child Labour and the Organisation of Production in the British Cotton Industry, 1780–1920* (Lund University Press, 1989) provides a meticulous explanation of these themes.

Chapter 2

# Child Slaves?
# Working children during the Industrial Revolution,
# c. 1780–1850

*Adam Booker, Leslie Willis, Jamie McHugh and Michael Winstanley*

## The coming of the factory system

'Whoever says Industrial Revolution says cotton';[1] we might add that whoever said cotton thought immediately of Lancashire. The textile industries of cotton and, to a lesser extent, wool increasingly dominated the economy of many parts of the county from the late eighteenth century, providing new experiences of employment for thousands of people, including children. To understand the changing nature of the work they did and the concerns it raised, it is first necessary to appreciate what the main developments in textiles were during this critical period.

Textile manufacture had long been an important occupation in Lancashire, but cotton was a relatively late arrival on the scene. By the middle of the sixteenth century, places such as Bolton, Bury, Burnley, Rochdale and Colne had begun to develop as small but important organising centres for the woollen manufacture dispersed in their surrounding areas, while centres in the south west of the county served the linen industry in similar ways.[2] The seventeenth century saw the emergence of fustians, a mixture of cotton and linen, and a widening domestic market for such cloth led to what some regard as a 'minor industrial revolution' over much of the county, especially around places like Blackburn and Bolton. Apart from the final stages of production, the work of cleaning, carding, spinning and weaving was largely carried out by hand in small workshops or the home, subsidizing the income of small farmers and cottagers, the women usually undertaking the spinning, the men the weaving, and the children providing such assistance as they could.

The eighteenth century saw major changes in textile production. This initially affected weaving, since John Kay's invention of the 'flying shuttle' in 1733 increased the speed and efficiency of weaving broadcloth by hand. This was followed in 1760 by the introduction of 'drop boxes' which allowed more than one shuttle to be in the loom ready for use, so that different cross-thread colours could be woven into the cloth. These improvements also increased productivity and therefore output, but they did not take work outside the home. Indeed, it is possible that by making the work less arduous, they allowed children to be more involved in the processes. Marjorie Cruickshank has suggested that 'by the age of twelve, as experienced weavers, they were responsible for carrying their own "cuts" to the middlemen, often a distance of several miles, and for bringing back their weft.'[3]

The increased productivity in weaving, however, meant that there was now a problem of supplying sufficient yarn, and it not surprising to find, therefore, that spinning saw the next wave of inventions. These led to the onset of the factory system and had a much greater impact on patterns of children's employment. In 1764 the 'spinning jenny' was invented by James Hargreaves. Initially this was a small machine, operated by one person turning a wheel which drove several spindles, so it was not incompatible with continued domestic production in the home, but it was later adapted to water and steam power. Before this, however, Richard Arkwright had invented a larger, more productive four-spindle, continuous spinning machine capable of producing a strong thread, using largely unskilled operators. More importantly, the machine could be powered by water, becoming known, therefore, as the 'water frame'. This meant that spinning began to move out of the home and groups of machines, sited initially in converted buildings, began to proliferate along water courses; the factory system had arrived.

This shift to factory production increased in pace from the 1770s, but was especially rapid after 1785 when Arkwright ceased to be able to enforce the rights to his patent. New mills emerged in many parts of east

Lancashire especially along the river tributaries that flowed down from the Pennines into rivers like the Tame, Roch, Calder, Irwell and Irk. In some areas there was a heavy concentration of mills along the same water course, as in the Shuttleworth valley north of Bury, where 'at least ten mills stood in the space of a mile'.[4] Among the largest of these early mills was the one on the River Bollin at Quarry Bank, Styal, just over the border in Cheshire, established in 1783 by the Greg family who were Manchester-based merchants who had been involved in contracting work out to domestic weavers, and who were anxious to diversify their business.[5] There were also significant numbers of early mills dispersed throughout the north and west of the county, along rivers like the Ribble and the Lune, with up to five factories at one time situated on tributaries at Caton to the east of Lancaster; one of them, Low Mill, established in 1783–4 in an old corn mill, later became part of the Gregs' business empire.[6] Another large early mill, specialising in calico printing and dyeing, was founded by Henry Fielding at Catterall near Garstang.[7] Further north still a mill was established at Backbarrow in Cartmel in 1782.[8]

Although some of these mills were in heavily populated areas, many were not, and their remote situations presented their owners with several problems, not least of which was labour. Since many had made heavy investment in spinning equipment, buildings, earthworks and water-powered machinery, they were reluctant to spend much on a labour force, either in wages or in the form of accommodation necessary to house workers in remote areas. Even in densely populated areas, the local people were sometimes reluctant to enter the mills, preferring the pattern of work associated with weaving at home; millowners especially in isolated areas sometimes had to import labour from elsewhere. These new workers were often children.

## Pauper apprentices

If there was a shortage of voluntary labour in parts of Lancashire, the same could not be said of some other parts of the country where parish authorities were struggling to find suitable employment for paupers and orphans and so remove the need to support them on local poor rates.[9]

Some of the local parishes supplied 'apprentices', but many came from further afield and advertisements were placed in northern newspapers by parishes offering children for employment. In *Wheeler's Manchester Chronicle* for 8 January 1775, for example, the overseers from Oswestry in Shropshire stated that, by applying to them, 'manufacturers and mechanics may be supplied with either boys or girls as parish apprentices from eight to sixteen years, all healthy children.'[10] The vicar of Biddulph, near Congleton, contacted Samuel Greg in 1817, writing, 'The thought has occurred to me that some of the younger branches of the poor of this parish might be useful to you as apprentices in your factory at Quarry Bank. If you are in want of any of the above, we could readily furnish you ten or more at from nine to twelve years of age.'[11] The largest supply, however, came from London and, a little later, Liverpool, where the problem was worst in poor working-class parishes. The mills at Backbarrow were at first worked almost entirely by children, 140 of them by 1805, drawn from the poor of the locality, and from as far away as London, Liverpool and Brighton.[12] Robert Peel, who had mills at Radcliffe, near Bury, was one of the largest employers of children with 1,000 on his books at one time.

It is difficult to conceive now of what life was like for such children in these mills. Conditions undoubtedly varied, but long hours, between twelve and fifteen per day, were everywhere the norm. Some mills even required children to work night shifts as well. Dr Aikin, a Manchester doctor writing in 1795 about conditions in Dukinfield, criticised 'the pernicious system . . . of making children in the mills work by night and day, one set getting out of bed when another goes into the same'.[13] Wages, if paid at all, were low, and apprentices would often work for little more than their board and lodging. Accommodation and care of the children out of work hours were always problems. Not all were like the Gregs who erected a purpose-built apprentice house. In one instance in the Rossendale Valley, children were boarded above the mill in a room which was so unsuitable that it collapsed.[14] Sometimes groups of children were only accepted if they were accompanied by a man and his wife to look after them, as was the case for paupers from a Hertfordshire workhouse engaged at a mill in Helmshore in Rossendale. They were also obliged to bring their own clothing, beds and bedding.[15]

The training they received was minimal, scarcely deserving the term 'apprenticeship', and it did not fit them for a future job in adult life; the contracts usually bound children until they were of age, but then discarded them in favour of more young recruits. In some instances they were dismissed during depressions when there was no work. The jobs they did were largely menial and repetitive: doffing (changing bobbins), piecing (putting broken threads together), scavenging for waste, cleaning the machines or sweeping up. With so many children under one roof, strict discipline had to be maintained, regardless of any allegations of cruelty. Fines, solitary confinement, reductions in diet, or physical punishment were all used to varying degrees. There were few restraints on the discipline of children transported from some distance away since they had no relatives to complain to, while local courts could find them guilty of 'disobeying the lawful commands of their master'. The conditions within the mill were also potentially harmful. Dr Aikin again commented that

> These children are usually too long confined to work in close rooms, often during the night; the air they breathe from the oil, &c., employed in the machinery and other circumstances is injurious; little regard is paid to their cleanliness, and frequent changes from a warm and dense to a cold and thin atmosphere, are predisposing causes to sickness and disability . . . and has debilitated the constitutions and retarded the growth of many.[16]

Aikin was not alone in expressing concern about the potential abuses involved in reliance on child labour. Following an outbreak of fever at Peel's Radcliffe mills in 1784, Manchester magistrates resolved not to allow 'indentures of Parish Apprentices whereby they shall be bound to owners of cotton mills and other works in which children are obliged to work in the night or for more than ten hours a day'.[17] Criticisms multiplied in the 1790s as parish authorities themselves began to express concern about the condition of the children they had apprenticed so far away from home. More and more began to impose conditions on apprenticeships, leading eventually to legislation in 1816 which curtailed London parishes' power to send children more than forty miles from the capital.[18] Even before that, Robert Peel had steered the 'Health and Morals of Apprentices Act' through Parliament in 1802. This limited hours to twelve per day, banned

night working for apprentices after 1804, and laid down regulations cover-
ing clothing, basic education, religious observance, dormitory accommodation, medical attention and conditions within the factory. Most
historians regard the Act as ineffectual since inspection and enforcement
was left to unpaid, local magistrates acting as district visitors, but it may
have hastened the trend, caused largely by technological change, to rely
more and more on local waged labour which was not subject to such
controls. However, some of the bigger rural millowners who found it
difficult to obtain local workers continued to rely on paupers, and when
labour became particularly short in the early 1830s the Gregs and Edmund
Ashworth of Turton, near Bolton, supported a scheme devised by Edwin
Chadwick, secretary to the Poor Law Commission, whereby pauper
families with large numbers of children were brought up from depressed
southern and eastern agricultural counties. The scheme proved very
unpopular, however, and by then most mills preferred to hire waged
labour from the local area.[19] Steam power and further changes in technology had heralded a new phase of factory development and different
patterns of employment.

## The 'Factory Question'

The successful application of steam power to cotton spinning gradually
replaced water as the main source of power in the early nineteenth
century. Its introduction allowed manufacturers to establish mills on
coalfields near to existing centres of population, reducing the need to rely
on imported pauper labour. The huge Manchester firm of McConnel and
Kennedy, for example, with a workforce of 1,125 in 1819, nearly half of
them under sixteen, never had to turn to apprentices.[20] Technology also
changed. Crompton's spinning mule produced a thread capable of being
used both for warp and weft. Initially the mule was hand-powered and
required more strength and skill from its operators, but with the application of steam it gradually replaced jennies and water frames. The perfec-
tion of a power loom in the 1820s capable of being driven by steam
sounded the death knell for domestic handloom weaving. Factory expansion was particularly rapid in the 1820s and the early 1830s by which time

yet more changes had been made to the mules. Longer mules, the practice of 'doubling up' whereby two existing machines were linked together, an increase in the number of spindles on each machine and the introduction of the 'self actor', which reduced some of the hard manual labour, all increased the number of spindles which could be controlled by an adult operator and his helpers.

Far from reducing the demand for child labour, however, such developments increased it. Although the responsibility for operating mules lay with adult male spinners or minders, children were still needed to assist them by doing a variety of jobs such as piecing broken ends together, doffing, cleaning and scavenging, while in weaving they were employed in similarly menial tasks, usually to help women who operated the looms. As the size of the mules increased and each adult was given responsibility for more of them, they required more youngsters to assist them. Whereas in the 1790s only one piecer per spinner was the norm, by the 1830s three piecers per spinner was not unusual. Most of these were hired and paid by the spinner himself out of what he earned from piece-work rather than by the manufacturer.

The employment of children in mills, woollen as well as cotton, created considerable controversy. The system was supported by manufacturers and writers like Dr Andrew Ure, Edward Baines of the *Leeds Mercury* and William Cooke Taylor who toured the manufacturing districts in 1842. Juvenile labour, according to Cooke Taylor, was a 'national blessing' since 'the children of the operatives have mouths and must be fed; they have limbs and must be clothed'.[21] Ure insisted that there was no maltreatment of children since 'No master would wish to have any wayward children to work within the walls of his factory, who do not mind their business without beating, and he therefore usually fines or turns away any spinners who are known to maltreat their assistants'.[22] Baines claimed that labour in the mills was far from onerous and compared well with other forms of work.[23] Ure, in his *Philosophy of Manufactures* (1835) painted a picture of a happy and prosperous workforce.

In my recent tour . . . through the manufacturing districts, I have seen tens of thousands of old, young and middle-aged of both sexes . . . earning abundant food, raiment, and domestic accommodation, without perspiring at a single pore, screened meanwhile from

Carding, drawing and roving.

the summer's sun and the winter's frost, in apartments more airy and salubrious than those of the metropolis in which our legislative and fashionable aristocracies assemble. In those spacious halls the benignant power of steam summons around him his myriads of willing menials, and assigns to each the regulated task, substituting for painful muscular effort on their part, the energies of his own gigantic arms, and demanding in return only attention and dexterity to correct such little aberrations as casually occur in his workmanship.[24]

Many political economists argued that for the state to interfere with the right of parents to decide what they should do with their own children was a gross infringement of individual liberty; it raised a very different principle than earlier legislation to protect pauper orphans from exploitation. The vast majority of manufacturers also vigorously opposed any restrictions, arguing that limitations of hours or other controls on their workforce would raise wage bills, increase prices, reduce demand and lead to the economic ruin of themselves and the country.

Long mule spinning.
In view of Edward Baines's enthusiasm for technological innovation, these representations (*opposite and above*) are not surprisingly dominated by the machinery which was transforming the cotton industry and portray deceptively spacious, clean interiors. Nevertheless, the artist has managed to illustrate some of the potential dangers of the factory for young workers, who are shown close to the unguarded cogs on the carding machines and 'sweeping under' the moving mules. (E. Baines, *History of the cotton manufacture in Great Britain.* London; Fisher, Fisher & Jackson, 1835. Fig 21, facing page 211 and Fig. 2.2, facing page 182)

But their arguments were countered by those anxious to prevent excessive exploitation of children. The Factory Act of 1819 prohibited children under nine from working in cotton mills and limited the work of those under sixteen to twelve hours per day, exclusive of meal times, but it left enforcement to local justices of the peace and most historians do not think that it was very effective. The campaign for stricter controls re-emerged in the early 1830s to abolish what Richard Oastler, a leading reformer, had claimed in a famous letter to the *Leeds Mercury* in 1830, was 'worse Slavery, and harder Bondage, than the Negroes in our *English* plantations in *America'*.[25] Within a few years a variety of groups had come together to call for controls, although often for very different reasons. Some were genuinely humanitarian, concerned with the moral and physical welfare of the children or worried that education and domestic training for girls were being sacrificed for short term profit. Doctors in the industrial districts in particular were often prominent in pointing out the physical evils of protracted factory work. Others, both Tories and working-class Radical political leaders, were perhaps more ideologically motivated, having no affection for the values of the new manufacturers and wishing to curtail their ability to acquire wealth and influence. Others looked back with affection to the days when work was largely done in the home, hoping that controls on factories would encourage a revival of the domestic system. Yet others felt that what they regarded as the 'natural order' of things was being inverted by conditions in factories with work for children and, especially in weaving, women, displacing that of the men, who should be the obvious breadwinners. Adult male spinners did not necessarily subscribe to this view, but their unions hoped that by curtailing the hours of children it would indirectly lead to shorter hours for adult workers since the mills would be forced to close earlier.[26]

The Factory Act of 1831 built on the earlier, limited legislation of 1819 by extending the restriction of twelve hours per day and nine on Saturday to young people under eighteen who worked in textile mills (excluding silk) and it prohibited night work for those under twenty-one. In 1833, after reports from a Parliamentary Select Committee and a Royal Commission, another Factory Act prohibited the employment of any children under nine and restricted those under thirteen to nine hours per day and forty eight per week while requiring them to attend a school for a minimum of two hours per day. A certificate from a local surgeon that a child appeared old enough and was fit to work was required before he or she could be taken on. For the first time, government inspectors were appointed to enforce the Act. Another Factory Act in 1844 introduced what became known as the half-time system. This reduced the age of minimum employment in textile mills from nine to eight but stipulated that children between eight and thirteen could only work either for six and a half hours per day and only then if they attended school for three hours daily between Monday and Friday, or for ten hours every alternate day, attending school

34

on the days on which they were not employed. Employers were given powers to deduct up to 2*d*. per week from children's wages to pay for the schooling and were obliged to obtain a certificate from a school teacher that the child had attended school during the preceding week. The Act also introduced minimum safety regulations. Further legislation in 1847, 1850 and 1853 fixed the times of day during which children and young persons could be employed and effectively introduced a ten-and-a-half-hour day for all workers.

Together these Acts marked a major shift in official attitudes towards child labour in factories. Instead of dealing only with paupers, those who had no parents or guardians to protect them, these applied to *all* children who worked in cotton, flax and woollen mills. How effectively the early acts were enforced has been a matter of some debate.[27] It has been suggested that parents who wished to put their children to work, manufacturers and spinners who wanted to employ them, surgeons who were paid to produce certificates, and magistrates who were charged with upholding the law, all disregarded the limitations on hours and ages, while the government-appointed inspectors were too few in number to enforce them. But recently some historians have suggested such a picture could be overdrawn and that prosecutions were also in fact much more common. By the 1850s both manufacturers and parents alike had come to accept the restrictions and the 'factory question' had apparently been effectively answered.[28] A sound system of regulation of children's work in the textile industries had been established which was to survive largely intact, with only minor amendments, up to 1918. The worst excesses had been abolished and young children were only able to work if they also attended school on a part-time basis (see chapter 3).

What we need to bear in mind, however, is that the intention behind such legislation was not to *prevent* children as young as eight from working but to *control* and regulate the work which they did. Some work was considered both necessary and desirable, but it was to be tempered by education. Furthermore, controls initially applied only to a limited range of industries which were considered to be exceptional: cotton, wool, flax and later, silk. The work of children in other trades was not affected, although it, too, from the early 1840s, became the subject of increasing scrutiny.

Growing concern about children's work in other trades found its expression in the Commission on Children's Employment which produced a series of reports in the early 1840s. This collected information from employers and workers throughout the country and appointed Assistant Commissioners to visit different regions. Inspections in Lancashire were largely carried out by Joseph Kennedy and Anthony Austin who each produced two reports, the first on mines in 1842 and the second on trades and manufacturing the following year.[29] These reports and the first-hand evidence they collected provide a vivid picture of the nature and extent of children's work and the issues which it raised, although, despite what we might see as the arduousness of the labour and the dubious condition of children thus employed, not all created the same levels of anxiety, and lack of work, especially in Liverpool, was viewed just as seriously.

## Handloom weaving and domestic industries

Kennedy's observations on conditions in handloom weaving serve as a reminder that conditions within the home might be no better and, in some instances, could be worse than in the new factories. Numbers in this trade fell dramatically from the 1820s as the power loom was introduced, but the shift to steam was not overnight and weaving by hand, especially of speciality, patterned, good quality cloth, often known as 'fancies', which could not yet be produced by power looms, continued over large parts of north-east Lancashire, around Bolton and along the Ribble valley into the third quarter of the nineteenth century.[30] In the township of Mellor, outside Blackburn, for example, it continued to be an important source of employment into the 1860s. (See Table 2.1)

For many families in Mellor weaving in the home sustained a 'family unit' and 'constituted a way of life that many did not want to relinquish'.[31] In south Lancashire, however, where handloom weavers were struggling unsuccessfully to compete with power looms in the weaving of coarser cloth, families were often in a state of desperate and increasing poverty, worse than that of any other artisan. Kennedy considered that 'the children . . . who are employed in this branch of manufacture at their own houses are more to be commiserated with than most of the operatives in

*Table 2.1*
*Children and handloom weaving: Mellor, 1861*

| Age | Boys | Girls | Total | % of age group employed |
|-----|------|-------|-------|-------------------------|
| 0–9 | 6 | 12 | 18 | |
| 10–14 | 31 | 25 | 56 | 41% |
| 15–19 | 34 | 46 | 80 | 62% |

Source: I. Holland, 'A Study of the Township of Mellor as a Handloom Weaving Settlement, using the Census Enumerators' Books' (unpublished M.A. dissertation, University of Lancaster, 1993), p. 62.

large manufactories'. He frequently found them working 'in cold, dark, damp cellars without any fire or means of ventilation and the atmosphere on entering the room was literally foetid with the breath of the inmates'. In theory they were at liberty to work what hours they pleased, but they were frequently forced by circumstance to work from five in the morning till twelve at night, yet only earning enough to keep them on a subsistence diet. In Kennedy's words,

it is one of those unhappy cases which it is impossible to reach by legislation and nothing remains but to warn the working classes to avoid entering upon an occupation which must for ever entail upon them an inheritance of disease and wretchedness.

Kennedy also commented briefly, but less critically, on other trades which were carried out at or near the home. Nail-makers around Leigh and Wigan employed their children from as young as eight or nine, but the work was open to the air and the hours were not long. However, they were 'swarthy and dirty in appearance' and the adults had the reputation of being 'ill-educated, drunken and profligate'. Hat-makers in Denton and Ashton-under-Lyne also worked in sheds attached to cottages, and 'in this manner they have their time entirely at their own disposal'.

# Mining

Kennedy also visited many of the coal mines at Burnley, Haslingden, Blackburn, Chorley, Hyde, Dukinfield, Stalybridge, the area around Wigan, and the south Lancashire mines owned by the Duke of Bridgewater. He interviewed over 800 workers about the ages at which they had started in the mine. The majority had begun work between the ages of six and eleven, although he considered that the age at which they were starting was going up and he detected a feeling that the miners themselves were increasingly averse to sending very young children, especially girls, down the mines. Boys had usually started work as door-tenders or trappers, opening air-doors to make way for waggons and closing them once they had passed, before 'graduating' to the job of drawer, gigger, thrutcher or waggoner. The job of door-tending he regarded 'as the most pitiable in the coal pit, from its extreme monotony', because 'the whole time is spent sitting in the dark for twelve hours . . . were it not for the passing of the waggoners it would be equal to solitary confinement of the worst kind'. Drawers were employed to drag coal underground in baskets from the face to the shafts but were only employed in the small mines with narrow seams; waggoners pulled or pushed trucks filled with coal for distances up to 500 yards. The age of these workers depended on the mine in question. Where seams were thicker and tramways were laid, 'young persons from fourteen to eighteen are preferred, as being stronger and better fitted for the work', but in mines where the seams were thinner, small children even as young as seven were employed. Boys as young as ten could also be employed as giggers, applying the brake to waggons; this job he regarded as 'tedious rather than laborious', and not too bad since, although 'these boys are also without light, . . . as they are in constant communication with the boys at the mouths of the different mines, their occupation is not so monotonous as that of the air door tenders'. Of particular concern, however, was the employment of children as engineers, that is in charge of machinery used to wind miners and coal to the surface, as this could cause accidents. John Halliwell, an overseer in Oldham, told Kennedy of a typical case. 'I remember a case two years ago, where a boy of ten years of age was managing an engine whilst five men were coming up, and he let the engine wind them over the head gear, and they were all killed.'

The hours worked by children employed in the coal mines were very variable but could be as long as from five in the morning until five in the evening or from six till six. The average working hours were 11 to 11½ per day, but they could be longer in winter when the demand for coal increased. Adults did not work this long as one witness, John Oldham from Outwood near Bolton, told Kennedy, 'a drawer will have to work near upon eleven hours per day; regular colliers will not work more than eight hours'. At least children did not usually work more than eleven days in a fortnight and often not more than ten days, as these were the days which the colliers kept. The Monday after pay-day was an informal holiday, often nicknamed 'Saint Monday', and in many mines no-one was expected to work that day.[32] In practice, many miners did not settle back into work until the middle of the week and the children, excluded from the drinking festival, would find themselves practically idle for two to three days. Kennedy expressed some concern over night work, but commented that this was only practised in a minority of Lancashire mines.

The drawers in a mine were more often than not employed by the colliers for whom they worked and this encouraged parents to employ their own children whenever possible. A collier was paid on the basis of the quantity of coal delivered from the coal face to the shaft and he had to pay for any cost incurred in this, so by employing his own children he kept the entirety of his wage for his own family. Kennedy noted that children's names did not appear in employers' workbooks and 'they never make their own contracts and their wages go to the general income of the family'. The air-door-tenders, giggers and other child labourers, however, were employed by the mine master and paid by the day, and thus had no contracts. The best children could earn from 3*d.* to 8*d.* per day. Any women or girls employed in a mine, of which there were very few, never graduated from being drawers and were only considered to be worth half a man's labour in the work they produced. Once the boys reached the age of eighteen they began to learn how to be colliers themselves.

Kennedy was concerned about the working conditions down mines. Most were very wet and later in life miners regularly developed rheumatism, heart disease and ophthalmia. Complaints such as ulcers, erysipelas and skin irritation were common. However, he was even more critical of miners' living conditions and morals. They rarely washed themselves

39

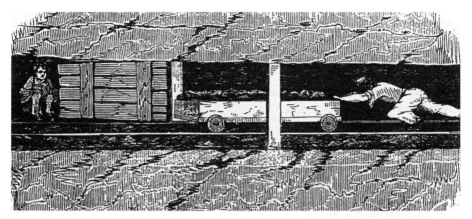

Air door tender and gigger in Lancashire mines.
Joseph Kennedy wrote of air door tending that 'Exertion there is none, nor labour, further than is requisite to open and shut a door. As these little fellows are always the youngest in the pits, I have generally found them very shy.' Giggers, managing the gig or balance on waggons, were also 'generally not more than ten years old' but their work involved more communication with others and was less lonely than that of the solitary door tender. (Reports from Commissioners (3) Children's Employment (Mines) PP. 1842, xvii; Fig. 2.3, page 166 and Fig. 2.4, page 167.)

beyond their faces and necks, and the children were 'exceedingly dirty'. Miners' homes were recognisable from 'the accumulations of filth and excrement at their doors, and by a savage bull-dog in the house'. The moral condition of miners and their children was equally deplorable, their 'ignorance and degraded moral state' being 'proverbial throughout this district' while 'want of education is accompanied by a degraded moral sense, gross and brutalized habits, depravity and crime'. These criticisms echo those made by some factory reformers, so it is not surprising that, by way of conclusion, he recommended that the regulations governing cotton mills be extended to mines because 'the interference was necessary for the protection of the children who were not able to protect themselves and also for the protection of the state from the growth of an ignorant, depraved and dangerous population'. The Mines and Collieries Act of 1842 banned females of any age and boys under ten from working underground but it did not include any provision for education.

## Other industries

Kennedy and Austin found few other trades where large numbers of children were employed and, with the exception of print works where the hours were long and irregular and the conditions far from healthy, they were not generally critical of the conditions they found. Children under fourteen were not generally employed in trades such as iron founding, machine-making, paper-making (Darwen), cloth printing, glass manufacture, and pipe-making (Prescot) or in bleaching and dyeworks. Much of the work was not considered injurious to health or morals. A few children were employed to grind and polish mirrors at St Helens and Warrington, but they did not handle mercury and the children in the plate glass works looked healthy. Those employed in bleaching 'looked remarkably healthy' and those in calendering were 'sprightly and in good health'.

Outdoor work was rarely criticised. Austin reported that in the slate quarries at Kirkby Ireleth the work was mainly above ground with children hired to drive carts around the sites. The work was similar at the copper mines at Coniston. Around Liverpool, he found that brick-making was a

A deliberately emotive portrayal from George Smith's polemical book, *The Cry of the Children from the Brickyards of England* (1871). Children's employment in Lancashire brickyards was not singled out as being particularly harmful by the Assistant Commissioners in the early 1840s. It was eventually regulated by the Factory and Workshop Act of 1867 but Smith continued to campaign for more stringent controls, drawing his evidence mainly from the Midlands. The Brickfield Act of 1871 subsequently legislated against the employment of girls under sixteen. (Frontispiece, 4th edn, J. & T. Spencer, 1871)

major seasonal employer of boys and a brick-maker, John Johnson, described the work which they did for him.

> There will be in Liverpool and neighbourhood 120 tables of bricks made or set up this year, and there will be 5 persons under 18 employed at each and 2 of them under 10 years of age. Their occupation is taking bricks from the table and wheeling them, and placing them on the ground to dry. It is hard work and they work long hours (from 4 in the morning till 9 in the summer, and as long as it is light in the other months).

Austin considered that the children in brickfields seemed to be in good general health, especially in comparison with the miners, and observed that the work was seasonal and well paid. Similarly Kennedy did not view the work which children as young as eight or nine did in nail-making around Leigh and near Wigan as too laborious; the hours were not considered excessive and much of the work was done in the open air.

Only a few industries attracted specific criticism from the commissioners. Austin described the pin-making industry at Warrington in some detail since the three major firms in the town between them employed the majority of the children, some 321. Boys and girls were both employed as pin-headers, but only girls were employed as pin-sheeters, putting the pins into sheets before they were packed away for delivery, 'because it was important that the pin-papers should not be spoiled by dirt, and girls were considered cleaner than boys'. Employment in the pin-works usually began between the ages of eight and twelve, although a few were reported as starting at a younger age. They worked from six or seven in the morning until eight at night but generally came and went as they pleased since they were paid on piece rates. They were considered for the most part to be badly fed, poor, weakly, delicate and feeble, but the conditions under which they worked in heated sheds in the poorest parts of town, although offensively close, were no worse, and possibly better than living conditions in their houses.

Austin also commented on works at Over Darwen where the refuse and sweepings of cotton mills were made into paper. Children worked long hours, from six in the morning until six at night with one and a half hours off work for meals, except for those who did not go home for meals, who worked through the breaks. In the three weeks before his visit, the works had been in operation day and night, with the night shift getting no allotted time for meals. Nevertheless, despite this tough regime, it seemed to Austin that the 'physical, as well as the moral condition of the young persons is good'.

## *Conclusion*

Austin's and Kennedy's reports are instructive, therefore, because they highlight the exceptional nature of the textile and mining industries and the concerns which they aroused during this period. Austin found very few children employed in towns like Ormskirk and very few in Lancaster outside cotton while 'in Liverpool there are many young children unemployed and, in fact, very few works in which it is advantageous to employ them'. However, neither were commissioned to give a complete picture of employment opportunities for children since they were instructed to comment only on places which employed relatively large workforces. Austin observed that 'works, trades or even retail shops where apprentices are taken are so numerous in the large towns' that he could only 'select those which seemed most to need investigation'. Kennedy commented that 'some of the worst cases of excessive employment of children . . . have been in occupations where they have been employed singly, or in the smallest numbers' and he condemned the apprentice system practised by small masters.

The commissioners' reports were somewhat different in tone and conclusions, but they both expressed common concerns about specific aspects of children's experiences. These anxieties echoed those made about work in textile factories. The possible effect of certain types of work on physical and moral condition was a major concern but for Kennedy in particular it was the neglect of education which work from a very early age entailed which was the primary concern, because it led to 'the growth of an ignorant and vicious population'. Idleness, however, was equally dangerous and restrictions on work, had to be accompanied by the provision of schooling. He concluded for the sake of education itself, measures which would lead to a total exclusion of children below the age of 13 rather than a limitation of their hours should be deprecated. A mixture of bodily labour and mental instruction being beneficial, I think it will, on due consideration, be found most desirable that they should be engaged in profitable employment part of every day.

Both Austin and Kennedy recognised, however, that poverty might deter parents from sending their children to school, and that the extension of education therefore depended partly on parents feeling prosperous enough to keep their children at school. Austin observed that 'Where the parents find work at reasonable wages they do not generally neglect to send their children to school, the "desideratum" is therefore to employ the parents'. The abolition of poverty, however, was unrealistic. Well into the twentieth century many parents would appear to have considered education an impediment to wage-earning and consequently they sent their children out to work as soon as they were allowed to.

For the next quarter century, therefore, legislation banned the employment of very young children in factories and workshops, but it controlled the conditions and restricted the hours of those aged over eight in specific trades while requiring them to receive some education. Not surprisingly, it was the model which had first been applied to textiles in 1833 and extended in 1844, combining part-time work with compulsory education and enforced by government-appointed inspectors, which was extended to other trades over the next quarter of a century.[33] This half-time system, however, was never as widely employed in these trades as it was in cotton and it is to its operation in cotton that we now turn.

*References:*

1. E. J. Hobsbawm, *Industry and Empire* (Penguin, 1969), p. 56.
2. For a detailed history of the early textile industry see A. P. Wadsworth and J. De L. Mann, *The Cotton Trade and Industrial Lancashire, 1600–1780* (Manchester University Press, 1931); for the later period, D. A. Farnie, *The English Cotton Industry and the World Market, 1815–1896* (Oxford University Press, 1979). J. K. Walton, Lancashire, 1558–1939: a social history (Manchester University Press, 1987) provides a long-term perspective and the social context.

3. M. Cruickshank, *Children and Industry: Child Health and Welfare in North-West Textile Towns during the Nineteenth Century* (Manchester University Press, 1981), p. 8.

4. O. Ashmore, *The Industrial Archaeology of Lancashire* (David & Charles, 1969), p. 43.

5. M. B. Rose, *The Gregs of Quarry Bank Mill: the Rise and Decline of a Family Firm, 1750–1914* (Cambridge University Press, 1986), pp. 13–18.

6. P. J. Gooderson, 'The Social and Economic History of Caton, 1750–1914' (unpublished M.A. dissertation, University of Lancaster, 1969), pp. 19–21.

7. C. Russell, *Lancastrian Chemist* (Open University Press, 1986), pp. 25–30.

8. T. E. H. Capper, 'The Rise and Decline of the Industrial Colonies at Backbarrow, Cark-in-Cartmel and Lowood, between the Eighteenth and the Twentieth Centuries' (unpublished M.A. dissertation, University of Lancaster, 1969), chapter 4.

9. M. B. Rose, 'Social Policy and Business: Parish Apprenticeship and the Early Factory System, 1750–1834', *Business History*, 31 (1989), pp. 5–26.

10. Rose, *Gregs of Quarry Bank Mill*, p. 30.

11. ibid., p. 31.

12. Capper, 'Backbarrow', chapter 4, p. 7.

13. Quoted in J. T. Ward, *The Factory System: vol. 1: Birth and Growth* (David & Charles, 1970), pp. 145–6.

14. Cruickshank, *Children and Industry*, p. 17.

15. ibid., p. 14.

16. Quoted in Ward, *The Factory System, vol. 1*, p. 145.

17. Quoted in B. L. Hutchins and A. Harrison, *A History of Factory Legislation* (P. S. King, 2nd edition, 1911), p. 9.

18. Rose, 'Social Policy', pp. 20–24.

19. *First Annual Report of the Poor Law Commissioners*, PP, 1835, xxix, p. 212.

20. C. H. Lee, *A Cotton Enterprise, 1795–1840: a history of McConnel & Kennedy, Fine Cotton Spinners* (Manchester University Press, 1972), pp. 115–24.

21. W. Cooke Taylor, *Notes of a Tour* (1842, repr. Frank Cass, 1968), p. 235.

22. A. Ure, *The Philosophy of Manufactures* (1835), quoted in J. T. Ward, *The Factory System vol. 2, The Factory System and Society* (David & Charles, 1970), p. 156.

23. Edward Baines, *History of the Cotton Manufacture in Great Britain*, (1835).

24. Quoted in Ward, *The Factory System, vol. 1*, p. 143

25. Quoted in H. Cunningham, *The Children of the Poor: Representations of Childhood since the Seventeenth Century* (Blackwell, 1991), p. 75.

26. The factory reform movement was too complex to be dealt with in this book; for some insight into it see J. T. Ward, *The Factory Movement, 1830–1855* (Macmillan, 1962) and the chapter in his edited collection, *Popular Movements, c. 1830–1850* (Macmillan, 1970), pp. 54–77.

27. A. E. Peacock, 'The Successful Prosecution of the Factory Acts, 1833–55', *Economic History Review*, 2nd series, xxxvii (1984), pp. 197–210; the debate between Peacock, Nardinelli and Bartrip in *Economic History Review*, 2nd. series, xxxviii, (1985), pp. 423–36.

28. R. Gray, 'The Languages of Factory Reform in Britain, c. 1830–1860', in P. Joyce (ed.), *The Historical Meanings of Work* (Cambridge University Press, 1987), pp. 143–79; Hutchins and Harrison, *Factory Legislation*, chapters 7 and 8.

29. *First Report of the Commissioners inquiring into the Employment and Condition of Children (Mines and Quarries)*. Reports with accompanying evidence on mining and quarrying in Lancashire, PP, 1842, xvii, pp. 149–92 (J. L. Kennedy) and pp. 787–818 (A. Austin); *Second Report of Commissioners (Trades and Manufactories)*, PP, 1843, xv, B1–B64 (Kennedy) and M1–M70 (Austin). All descriptions of domestic industry, mining and manufacturing in the next three sections are drawn from these reports and accompanying evidence unless otherwise stated. Joseph Fletcher also submitted a report on collieries around Oldham, PP, 1842, xvii, pp. 819–36.

30. D. Bythell, *The Handloom Weavers* (Cambridge University Press, 1969); G. Timmins, *The Last Shift: the Decline of Handloom Weaving in Nineteenth-Century Lancashire* (Manchester University Press, 1993).

31. Timmins, *Last Shift*, p. 121; Holland, 'Mellor', p. 67.

32. For a fuller explanation of the Lancashire tradition of 'Saint Monday' see Walton, *Lancashire*, pp. 82, 98.

33. A. H. Robson, *The Education of Children Engaged in Industry in England, 1833–1876* (Kegan Paul, 1931) provides a full description of this process.

Chapter 3

# 'No school, no mill; no mill, no money': the half-time textile worker

*Hilary Challand and Michael Walker*

THE factory legislation of the nineteenth century sought to curb the exploitation of children and ensure that those aged eight or above who worked received *some* education. Since it did not ban their employment, children continued to represent a large proportion of the workforce. This was especially noticeable in the cotton towns of mid- and east Lancashire, where the half-time system established in 1844 remained an integral part of growing-up until after the First World War. Working-class parents often saw little benefit in continued education and many families, especially in weaving areas of Lancashire, relied on the incomes of their children to keep them above the poverty line. It was frequently the case that as soon as children were, or looked, old enough, they would be found a place in the mill, as people who remember their early years often recall. One who worked in a cotton factory in Preston remarked that 'them days we had to go in the mill. You weren't asked'.[1] It was often part of a family tradition, as a man who worked half-time as late as 1916 described: 'Your family would plan it. It was just a matter of what mill you went to. You always went to a mill where you had a relation so you relied on a relation taking you.'[2]

## The development of the half-time system

Factory workers were the first children in the country for whom *some* education was compulsory, but among the last required to attend *full-time* up to the age of fourteen. Legislation requiring pauper apprentices to receive education dated back to 1802, and the Factory Act of 1833 also included some provision for those between nine and thirteen inclusive, but the half-time system, as it soon became known, was effectively brought in by the Factory Act of 1844.[3] This tried to balance the needs of education and industry, as well as introducing safeguards designed to promote safety at work and prevent excessive hours.[4] Among those concerned about young workers' educational standards had been Leonard Horner, the factory inspector appointed after the 1833 Factory Act with responsibility for most of the northern textile district, and he had been fully involved in the writing of the preceding Royal Commission's recommendations. Under the provisions of the 1844 Act, children employed in textile factories (except silk), aged between eight and thirteen, were allowed to work either ten hours per day on three days per week, attending school full-time for the alternating days; or six and a half hours per day, every working day (i.e. six days a week), while attending school for three hours each day except Saturday. In order to work, half-timers had to produce a certificate of school attendance for the preceding week. Any shortfall in stipulated school hours had to be made up before paid work could be allowed, so there was a very real incentive to maintain good attendance and, since there were no requirements to send children who did not work to school, it was possible that children might only have started attending when they began in the mills in order to allow them to work. As the Darwen children's chant put it, 'No school, no mill; no mill, no money'.[5] For these reasons, there were discrepancies in the ages children actually went half-time; if they could be passed off as older, they were.

The half-time system in textile factories soon came to be considered as the ideal model to be applied to other workplaces which employed children; it combined the benefits of education with early training for work.[6] Evidence seemed to suggest that half-timers performed better at school than full-timers did; an inspector of schools writing to Horner explained why.

49

The question naturally occurs, how is it that children who attend school for three hours a day only are equal in attainments to those who are able to attend for six hours a day. I answer that the *regularity* of their attendance compensates for the fewer hours. The attendance of the children of the labouring classes at our national schools is very irregular. The half-timer is never absent on a school day; he keeps adding line upon line; and he is not allowed to forget the last lesson.[7]

An official enquiry of 1862 suggested that in all the textile districts of the United Kingdom in 1856 there were an estimated 46,071 half-timers and of this total, 14,000 'would never have been sent to school by parental affection and consideration unless they had been employed in the factories'.[8] The system, therefore, was extended to other occupations and industries: print works (1845), bleaching and dyeing (1860), lace factories (1861), pottery, match-making, percussion caps and cartridges and fustian cutting (1864) and then, in the Factory Act of 1867, to virtually all non-textile factories and workshops.

After the Education Acts of 1870 and 1876, however, which established local School Boards and School Attendance Committees and gave them discretion to make full-time education compulsory to the age of ten years, matters became more complicated and attitudes began to change. Half-timers were initially exempt from full-time provisions, but the idea of requiring compulsory education to the age of ten gained popularity. Since the anomaly seemed to be encouraging more parents to send their children half-time, the loophole was closed by the 1874 Factory Act which raised the minimum age at which a child could go part-time to ten to take effect from 1876. This Act also raised the age at which any children could work full-time to fourteen, unless they were able to pass a certain 'Standard' laid down by the school authorities or accumulate a given number of attendances, in which case they could obtain exemption at thirteen. The Elementary Education Act of 1876 allowed boards and committees to fix the standards appropriate to their localities. The 1891 Factory Act raised the minimum age for employment in factories to eleven, and the Education Act of 1893 raised the school leaving age to this where it remained until 1899, when it was again raised, this time to twelve, from 1 January 1900. The system was only finally swept away by the 1918 Education Act which abolished all partial exemptions and established compulsory, full-time schooling until a child's fourteenth birthday.

The numbers of children employed as half-timers and the jobs they did varied over the nineteenth century. Precise numbers of half-timers in Lancashire at any one time are difficult to compile. Some schoolchildren were registered as qualified half-timers but were not necessarily at work and continued to attend full-time. Official figures and those reproduced in books on the subject often related to the whole country or to all textiles, not just cotton, or referred to all children who were registered as half-timers any time during a year, rather than those employed on a specific day, clearly inflating the total number at work. However, it would seem that numbers expanded up to the 1870s but declined thereafter as the minimum age limit was raised, although there were some temporary reversals in this trend. In 1875 there were 67,000 half-time children in the cotton industry, mainly in Lancashire, of which total Blackburn claimed the highest number at 6,000. In 1892 over 170,000 half-timers were registered in the country, and over half of them, 89,000, were in Lancashire, the overwhelming majority in cotton. The raising of the age at which a child could go half-time in the 1890s led to a fall nationally to just over 110,000 by 1897 and only 47,000 by 1906, but another source suggests that the figure had risen to over 70,000 by 1911–12. The fall was more noticeable in other industries, however, and the proportion of the national total who were employed in Lancashire cotton actually rose during the same period.[9] A boom in the cotton industry in the mid 1900s actually led to an increase in numbers employed for a number of years. It was also reported that more children were obtaining exemptions to leave school completely at thirteen rather than go part-time at twelve.

Nationally the proportion of the cotton workforce who were children rose from around 4.6 per cent in 1850 to peak at 14 per cent in 1874 before declining to 9.1 per cent in 1890; it fell still further in the next two decades.[10] But this disguises the fact that the jobs the children did changed over the period. In the early decades they were primarily employed in spinning, but they were to become increasingly important in weaving where they rose from under one per cent of the workforce in 1850, to 13.5 per cent in 1874 and 'their numbers would have increased even faster if the minimum age for half-timers had not been raised in 1874'.[11] From the 1880s specialised weaving firms of north-east Lancashire were most dependent on children and remained so until after 1918. This is confirmed by an investigation into half-time rates at fifteen primary schools in Accrington Borough which suggests that in the years leading up to the First World War around 10 per cent of the entire school roll, amounting to virtually all the top form in many schools, were in half-time work.[12] The situation was similar in Blackburn although in schools in spinning towns like Oldham rather fewer were involved. By the age of 13, however, the majority of children had left entirely.

*Table 3.1*
*Full- and half-timers on school registers in Oldham and Blackburn, 1909*

| Town | School | 12–13 year-olds | | 13–14 year-olds | |
|------|--------|------|------|------|------|
| | | Full-time | Half-time | Full-time | Half-time |
| Blackburn | Christ Church C.E. | 19 | 73 | 5 | 21 |
| Blackburn | Bank Top Council School | 7 | 28 | 4 | 7 |
| Blackburn | St Albans R.C. | 25 | 67 | 18 | 12 |
| Oldham | Derker Council School | 77 | 81 | 25 | 11 |
| Oldham | Northmoor Grange St. | 54 | 64 | 9 | 10 |
| Oldham | St Patrick's R.C. (boys) | 22 | 19 | 6 | 2 |
| Oldham | St Patrick's R.C. (girls) | 57 | 14 | 6 | 1 |

Source: *Inter-Departmental Committee on Partial Exemption from School Attendance*, PP, 1909, xvii, pp. 1018–22.

Table 3.2, based on the census of 1911, shows that very high proportions of half-timers were to be found in all the weaving districts; figures were somewhat lower in spinning towns but were still well above the national average of children employed. In most of these areas, the number of attendances or the standard which a child had to attain before he or she could go half-time was fixed deliberately low. The absence of some towns from the list reflects a much more rigorous approach which the authorities there adopted. In Bury, for example, the council reserved the right to refuse half-time certificates unless a child would be 'necessarily and beneficially employed', which effectively meant that parents had to prove poverty and show that their child had an acceptable job to go to. Similar conditions did not apply to full-time exemption from the age of thirteen, however, so many still left before the official leaving age of fourteen.

*Table 3.2*
*Percentages of twelve year-olds in employment: Lancashire, 1911*
*Urban Districts and Boroughs with more than 50 per cent occupied (boys or girls)*

| District/Borough | Status | Boys | Girls |
|---|---|---|---|
| Bacup | mb | 68 | 51 |
| Barrowford | ud | 68 | 62 |
| Brierfield | ud | 68 | 56 |
| Great Harwood | ud | 66 | 68 |
| Crompton | ud | 64 | 53 |
| Darwen | mb | 63 | 58 |
| Milnrow | ud | 63 | 57 |
| Oswaldtwistle | ud | 60 | 52 |
| Rishton | ud | 60 | 49 |
| Rawtenstall | mb | 58 | 49 |
| Nelson | mb | 56 | 49 |
| Walton-le-Dale | ud | 56 | 61 |
| Clayton-le-Moors | ud | 54 | 55 |
| Haslingden | ud | 53 | 44 |
| Colne | mb | 52 | 40 |
| Leyland | ud | 51 | 39 |
| Whitworth | ud | 51 | 36 |
| Padiham | ud | 50 | 43 |
| Accrington | mb | 50 | 45 |
| Little Hulton | ud | 50 | 52 |

ud = urban district, mb = municipal borough
Source: *Census of Great Britain, 1911*; Lancashire, Table 26.

## Duties and wages: piecers and tenters

The main processes in the cotton industry operated on a piece-work basis, with adult workers being paid according to the amount which they produced. A system of sub-contracting existed which meant that many child workers, instead of being directly employed by the manufacturer, were employed by adults and paid out of their wages. Not all children were employed this way, but it was common in the main processes involved in spinning and weaving.

The jobs undertaken by half-timers were very similar to those which young children did once they had left school completely. It is not possible to describe them in detail, since they covered virtually all the stages of production. The work, however, was invariably the least skilled and most monotonous. Some jobs like 'scavenging', the cleaning of the machinery and floors, were common to all sections of the industry and an Act of 1878 expressly forbade this practice while the machines were in motion. Children were also frequently employed in jobs like oiling the machinery and wiping down twice daily, as the machines powered down for the midday break and evening close-down. Any oil was carefully wiped away, along with cotton waste or fluff. While the machines were running smoothly a host of sundry jobs could be done, unrelated to the machinery, including replenishment of the fire water-buckets, which were often used for hand-washing after visits to the privy, making tea for adults, or getting their dinner at mid-day.[13]

Children, however, also undertook jobs related to specific processes. 'Carding' was a process designed to prepare the cotton wool for spinning and it employed a machine which laid cotton fibres flat and parallel by means of hundreds of tiny metal barbs, producing a 'card web' – an almost transparent film of fibres. Renewal of the metal cans receiving the resulting 'slivers' or thick, loose ropes of cotton was undertaken about every fifteen minutes and was invariably performed by women or children.[14] The tiny metal barbs used by this equipment were also replaced as necessary and a hand inserted too far into the machine could result in loss of finger tips. Copious quantities of dust were thrown out, liable to be breathed in. 'Drawing' was accomplished by a machine which combined 'slivers' of carded cotton, with a slight strengthening twist, from the metal cans into a finer coil or 'roving' which could then be used in spinning. These needed frequent replenishment, so the job of 'carrying the can' was often devolved to half-timers.

'Creeling' involved regularly supplying and fitting new roving to the spinning-mule spindles. Then there was the seemingly never-ending job of 'piecing' which involved the repair of threads broken during the

A little piecer sweeping up in Oldham, c. 1900. The essentials of the job had
changed little since the 1830s. Despite legislation banning sweeping up while
machines were in motion, critics like Allen Clarke in his *The Effects of the Factory
System* (1899) claimed that it was still practised 'with a dexterous rush that
compels admiration; but a moment's carelessness, a second's miscalculation,
means a frightful injury'. Spinners and piecers worked barefooted to give a
better grip on the oil-stained floor. (Oldham Metropolitan Borough Leisure
Services, Local Studies Library)

mule-spinning process. Catling reckoned that 'on a pair of typical late
period mules of 1,200 spindles each, about five or six ends would be
breaking each minute. Clearly the work of repairing broken ends could
never be neglected for more than a few minutes and was a most important
staple task.'[15] A 'sawney', the simultaneous breakage of every thread in
the mule, created much consternation and hectic remedial attention, often
with the assistance of friends from elsewhere in the factory.[16] Young
children, boys and girls, were often referred to specifically as 'little piecers';
'big piecers' were older youths who combined many of the more routine

55

Carding machines.

Two postcards (*above and opposite*) from a series published around the turn of the century illustrating the various stages of cotton production. Carding was predominantly men's work, although young lads were employed to assist them. Boys and girls were both employed in weaving. The gentle remonstrance of the weaver and his non-threatening stance fosters a more attractive image of the workplace than that of the solitary little piecer (page 55). (Lancashire County Library, Burnley Local Studies Collection)

spinning operations on a training basis with their piecing duties. 'Doffing' involved taking from the spinning mules full cops (conical windings of yarn) and replacing them with empty ones. This was often only necessary once or twice per day. Children might also be involved in carrying the full skips of spun yarn (following a doffing), to the cellarman's hoist, a job which required strong shoulders.[17]

Some regarded such work in spinning as relatively light, but others were more critical. J. R. Clynes, who became a dominant campaigner for the abolition of the half-time system,[18] worked as a 'little piecer' in the Dowry Mill at Oldham and graphically described in emotional terms the dangers of a piecer's job. 'Often the threads on the spindles broke as they were

56

'Tha'll hav' to do diff'rent to this'.

stretched and twisted and spun. These broken ends had to be instantly repaired; the piecer ran forward and joined them swiftly, with a deft touch.' When he fell, he recalls 'rolling instinctively and in terror from beneath the gliding jennies, well aware that horrible mutilation or death would result if the advancing monsters overtook and gripped me'.[19] Oiling the spindles also had to be performed at a crucial time, between the first movement of the overhead shafting and settling-in of the machinery at a given speed, and the oil had to be applied in precise amounts; too little would cause overheating of the bearings; too much would result in excess oil being thrown off as the spindles speeded up, staining the weft. A hazard of this oil was the potential development, over time, of cancer of the scrotum (frequently called spinner's cancer). Mineral oil was implicated as the cause, coming into contact with clothing when workers leaned forward against oil-spattered machinery to make running adjustments. A fine oil mist-spray was given off by the rapidly rotating spindles, staining any person in the near vicinity. By the end of a working day, clothing could be badly affected by oil which penetrated fibres, finally coming into contact with the skin.[20]

In weaving children often worked in weaving as 'tenters', watching over looms while learning the job, pointing out to the weaver if anything untoward developed. By these means an adult weaver could run many looms, attending to each in succession or as necessary, and the half-time system meant, for example, that a weaver could employ a different child in the morning and afternoon, their assistance enabling him, or her, to operate six looms instead of four, thus increasing earnings.[21] The tenter would also perform routine duties such as refilling the shuttles with weft, which involved a process known as 'kissing' the shuttle, and obtaining fresh supplies of weft when required. As in spinning, repairing threads, this time in the loom, was an important aspect of the job which had to be done skilfully so as to create a minimal effect in the finished cloth.[22] All this was done while the machines were working; as a former Preston half-timer recalls, 'they wouldn't stop their looms hardly to piece ends'.[23]

Recollections of such work are mixed. A former girl half-timer remembered that while they were learning they had to 'go in the warehouse for the weft . . . take the cuffs that she had already woven when [they were] pulled out of the rollers, [and] carry [them] in the warehouse and have them checked in'.[24] Another commented that it was 'a terrible life it was really. The things you had to do, it was hard work. You used to have to sweep your looms and clean your looms and go and lay on a flagged floor and sweep underneath your looms.'[25] Not all, however, were so critical; work was potentially much more interesting and rewarding than school, or doing nothing. 'I thought it was wonderful'.[26]

Surprisingly, half-timers did not always receive wages for the work they did and could often spend several months classed as 'learners'. The Inter-Departmental Committee on Partial Exemption from School Attendance in 1909 contained details of half-timers in schools and Blackburn, Burnley and Oldham which clearly shows this to be the case. Among the 94 half-timers at Christ Church School Blackburn, for example, were 16 who worked for family members, and 39 who were 'learning'; only 35 were listed as receiving wages. At Bank Top School only 15 of the 35 half-timers received wages. Tenters by this date usually received 2s. 9d. per week; boys engaged in the warehouse 3s. and winders 4s. Fewer children, 15 out of 92, were recorded as learners in Derker School, Oldham, and none was listed as working for relatives. Weavers here received about 2s. 9d., about the same as ring spinners and doffers, while piecers earned between 3s. and 4s., presumably depending on skill. When children did receive wages, therefore, their income could be crucial for the family budget.[27]

## Voices in favour

For a long time, the half-time system was generally viewed favourably by all concerned; the ageing Edwin Chadwick, who had been instrumental in promoting legislation in 1844, was still defending its record as late as 1880.[28] But from the 1880s, the system aroused increasingly strong passions and arguments. Critics of the half-time system were often educated and literate, and they were able to ensure that their views were widely circulated so that historians have tended to take most notice of them. But there were many in favour of its retention whose views are often overlooked because they were not able to publicise them as effectively. These were primarily the parents/guardians of the working children, the textile unions representing adult workers, and the manufacturers, especially the weavers. The editorial and letter columns of the *Cotton Factory Times*, the official organ of the cotton unions, which was published weekly throughout this period, provided an opportunity for those with an interest to voice their views. As the bill to raise the half-time age from eleven to twelve years was going through the various parliamentary stages in 1899, opinions were freely and forcibly expressed in the newspaper's columns. They provide a vivid insight into the attitude of the cotton industry workforce at this time, giving a voice to individuals often otherwise ignored in the historical record.

A group of weavers captured by the camera outside a mill in Nelson just prior to the First World War. Note the girls' shawls. (Lancashire County Library, Burnley Local Studies Collection)

With half-timers earning between 2s. 6d. and 4s. per week at the time, many parents, in the weaving areas in particular, regarded their children's income as essential to the maintenance of a decent living standard for the family. Widows were often portrayed particularly poignantly, with their children employed half-time providing their only visible means of support and preventing the dreaded entry through the workhouse door. One line of argument, therefore, was that without half-time work there would be more applicants for parish relief. The widely acknowledged problems of 'street urchins' in Liverpool were also held up as an example of the affliction which might affect the textile towns if half-time work were curtailed.[29] Individuals wrote letters to the paper voicing these opinions. John Hargreaves of 11 Clement Street, Accrington, for example, wrote on 6 January 1899:

> The half-timer is taking no harm, he is better clothed and fed than thousands of the poor children who inhabit our large cities (places

which, by the way, scorn the idea of the half-timer, through ignorance of his true condition). His better condition is brought about to a great extent by his own earnings, and if the age is now allowed to be raised to 13, as proposed, depend upon it the same arguments will be used by the same class of people (certainly not by practical persons) to raise the age still higher, to say, 15 or 16.

Similarly James Bleakley of 262 Blackburn Road, Bolton, wrote on a number of occasions about the matter. On 20 January he called for the 'immediate repeal of its [Education Act] draconic penal laws against the "derelict" poor operatives and their starving families, who are deprived of what their children might be able to earn by honest labour to keep body and soul together. 8000 prosecuted in Bolton, 1,860,000 in England & Wales.'[30] He continued in a similar vein later in the year.

You cannot with truth deny that the half-timer's bill is a deliberate national imposture, increasing the tyranny and persecution of the poor . . . Perish your education which does not teach the children how they may prosper themselves, their homes and their country by working, and how to get it, and how to avoid being imposed upon and ruined body and soul by false teachers, unprincipled guides and leaders.[31]

Furthermore, writers argued that the principle of freedom of choice for the individual was at stake in this. They pointed to the long-standing argument that if workers' labour was their only asset, they should not be prevented from using such an asset to their best advantage.

As this implies, a common line was to attack the bill as promoting the selfish interest of those in education; it was sometimes referred to as the 'schoolmasters' increase of wages bill'.[32] This is an allusion to the fact that each morning or afternoon school session attendance generated a grant from the government to the school. Naturally, with fewer half-timers and more full-timers, attendance rates and school grants would increase. An anonymous columnist also suggested that this led to more widespread discrimination against half-timers.

The schoolmaster regards the half-timer simply as a grant-earner. Regretting that he does not come full-time, he will not take pains to teach the lad and encourage the pupil-teacher to take pains with him. If any of the boys get into trouble, and the half-timer is amongst them, the punishment or whacking is meted out heavily to the half-timer, while a light punishment only is given to the full-timer. This is because they are aware that to thrash the full-time boys might cause them to leave the school and go to another; but the half-timer is bound to keep at his own factory school, and therefore cannot change schools. He becomes a 'little slave' to the schoolmaster . . . It is well-known that there is a ban put upon the half-timer gaining any of the [school] prizes.[33]

Further arguments expressed concern about the likely cost of increased school provision,[34] and portrayed schools as 'little prisons' in comparison to healthy, 'airy' factories.[35] No letters gave an opposing view in the year leading up to the implementation of the Act on 1 January 1900 and the editorial opinion in the *Cotton Factory Times* also clearly supported half-time working.

Cotton unions also opposed the raising of the school age as published results of workers' ballots show. The Amalgamated Association of Beamers, Twisters and Drawers of Lancashire, Derbyshire, Cheshire & Yorkshire recorded an overwhelming majority against any alteration of the present age limit, arguing that 'In this branch of the textile trade it is considered impossible to dispense with child labour'.[36] Similarly, the Bolton & District Cotton Spinners' Association, consisting of members in Bolton, Chorley, Atherton, Tyldesley, Hindley, Manchester, Salford, Reddish, Pendlebury, Patricroft, Farnworth, Horwich, Turton and Westhoughton, voted almost universally against the bill, 8,201 votes being in favour and 66,316 against.[37]

During the year the paper carried various articles to underline the apparent perversity of the proposed and imminent increase in half-time age at a time when labour was allegedly already short.

| | |
|---|---|
| 6 January: | Darwen – 'Scarcity of Tenters'. |
| 13 January: | Rochdale – 'Scarcity of Little Piecers'. |
| 30 June: | 'The question of obtaining a full supply of little piecers for spinning mills is becoming rather a serious one, and is giving a deal of trouble in more ways than one.' |

28 July:                'At the present time a good deal of extra labour is put upon minders owing to scavengers being so scarce.'
25 August 1899:   'A phenomenal scarcity of piecers'.

The issue dated 1 September 1899 carried the following announcement urging parents to apply immediately if they wished their children to go part-time.

*The New Half-Time Bill – An Important Warning:*

On and after January next no child will be allowed to go half-time under twelve years of age. Those parents who desire to have their children half-timers under the present Act should at once see that they are entered for the next labour examination . . . as soon as a child has passed . . . and received a certificate to that effect, the parent can then apply for a half-time certificate.

The final issue for 29 December 1899 reminded readers in a rather regretful tone of the new act coming into force from 1 January.

It is likely that the *Cotton Factory Times* reflected the feelings of many cotton workers who continued to oppose further erosion of the system right up to 1918. While there were no contributions from the employers, it is fair to assume that their silence amounted to a tacit acquiescence in the sentiments expressed, because they, too, continued to defend the system elsewhere against its attackers. The views of the children themselves were rarely heard in all of this, but it is quite probable that many of them also approved of a system which allowed them to reduce their attendance at school and gave them an opportunity to earn money. The Inter-Departmental Committee on Physical Deterioration reported in 1904 that

The children themselves like going to the mills. At first, at any rate, they enjoy the sense of being grown up and independent, and of having money to spend. We were not surprised to hear of a case where out of three hundred children questioned only seven replied that they would have preferred not to have gone into the mill.[38]

## Critics

Arguments against the half-time system often focused on the educational problems which it raised, with well-reported difficulties which the children encountered in 'competing with a child who was having twice as much education without the burden of manual work'.[39] Although the system had initially been established to give the child worker more access to education, by the end of the century, once full-time schooling was the norm, it meant that they received less than other children. Half-timers were expected to participate fully in lessons alongside full-timers, but it was frequently reported, for example by Margaret Macmillan during her visit to the worsted town of Bradford, where the half-time system was extensively used, that many had difficulty even staying awake, especially in the afternoons after they had worked a morning shift. Children who only

Young weavers at George Street Manufacturing Company's Coronation Mill, Burnley, *c.* 1912. Their hair is tied back to lessen the danger of catching it in the machinery; 'letting one's hair down' naturally implied being at leisure. (Lancashire County Library, Burnley Local Studies Collection)

attended half-time were often regarded as backward, which was probably not the case; they simply had less chance to learn.

Half-time posed problems for school teachers and governors alike. *The Schoolmaster*, a journal supported by the National Union of Teachers, regularly carried articles criticising the system. One in 1884, entitled 'In Clog Land – The Troubles of the Half-Timer', outlined the difficult circumstances which teachers were placed under. They could not organise a timetable which would prepare every pupil for the Inspectors' examination. It was 'almost an impossibility and at best a highly unsatisfactory affair . . . . [The] work of the Monday afternoon is repeated on the Tuesday morning, and so on during the week, with an ever changing set of pupils who are able to pick up their humble scraps of knowledge in a way at once tantalising and unsatisfactory'.[40] The paper argued that, as a result, the children received a very poor education, or hardly any at all; there was a waste of precious resources with expensive teaching directed at tired, unresponsive children.[41] The situation was made worse by the fact that grants to schools were based upon the number of attendances and the results of examinations: this was the 'payment by results'[42] system which made no allowance for half-timers, who consequently earned less money for the school. Yet the paperwork involved in confirming half-time attendance was a considerable fatigue for the teachers in the schools involved. The head teacher of Accrington Union Street school regularly committed his feelings on the subject to the school log book until he delegated the task to his assistant.[43]

Contemporary criticisms are echoed by some of those who recall being at school at the time. One commented, 'They couldn't teach a half-timer anything. If you had the same subject morning and afternoon, they got the morning one and missed the afternoon one. How on earth could they catch up with you?'[44] Another man who worked as a half-timer in Preston recalls that teachers treated such as he with less respect than day scholars. 'They didn't seem to bother the same after you went half-time, the teachers lost interest in you. It was a handicap because they could be having a lesson in the morning while I was at work then they would continue with it in the afternoon. Well you didn't know anything about it. So they had you up as a bad egg really.'[45] Other writers suggested that their allegedly dirty, foul-smelling clothes made half-timers unwelcome classmates.[46] Oral recollections sometimes refer to this: 'I used to have one lad sat next to me and he was an absolute dunce . . . he could neither read, write nor add up . . . and they [the half-timers] would stink to high heaven.'[47]

In more general terms, there were criticisms that, starting work at a tender age as they did, half-timers were considered to be exposed to moral risks, including smoking and bad language. Consequently they were thought to be rude, unruly and abusive. The study carried out by *The Schoolmaster* in 1884 suggested that the half-timers needed to be controlled with strong discipline, a teacher from Oldham reporting that they 'had a tendency to a brusqueness of manner and generally, indeed, to be a source of trouble if not ruled with a strict hand'.[48]

From the factory perspective, a half-time child having attended the morning session at school, cannot have been fully productive or alert. Lack of concentration, a handicap in class, was potentially fatal in a factory. Some observers also felt that children of tender years were not 'free agents' – they could not stand up for themselves in the real world and were hence liable to exploitation.[49] There were also many criticisms of the type of work which half-timers did. Their jobs were very demanding, they had to be alert at all times because the machines could cause fatal injuries in surroundings which, despite legislation imposing safety measures, were still far from safe. J. R. Clynes, describing his job as a piecer, painted a particularly unpleasant picture of the conditions he worked under.

I performed it, unresting, in my bare feet . . . . Sometimes splinters as keen as daggers drove through my naked feet leaving aching wounds from which dribbles of blood oozed forth to add to the slipperiness of the floor. I just had to try to avoid the splinters and the falls; there were few chances to tear the jagged bits of wood away while those unprotected machines were on the move . . . . My ten year old legs felt like lead and my head spun faster than the pitiless machinery. But I had to keep on; the dinner whistle would shrill some time soon; then I could rest aches and regain my breath, ready to run two miles home to dinner, and then set off for school.[50]

He considered school little better, however, but for different reasons, arguing that the method of teaching seemed to 'prevent me from thinking for myself'.

Allen Clarke, who had experienced life first as a piecer and then as a teacher for eight years (suggestive perhaps that it was possible for half-timers to learn something!), was another who publicly campaigned against the system. The 'premature sharpness' which he thought some half-timers exhibited, soon 'stupefies into the dull automatism common to factory folk, who toil but think not'. Half-time work also 'stunted their growth'. The work they did was highly dangerous since much of the 'sweeping up' under the machines was done while they were in motion, despite legislation which had banned it in 1878. Parents and the adult piece workers who employed the children were the main culprits, he concluded. 'Wage is more valuable than life or limb of man, woman or child.'[51]

Clynes and Clarke were among the prominent socialists who campaigned against the half-time system from the 1890s onwards. Many also maintained, however, that it should not be abolished until state maintenance (i.e. welfare support) was introduced to support families. Dan Irving, organiser of the Social Democratic Federation (S. D. F.) in Burnley, took this stance in the 1880's. He proposed that the exploitation could only be stopped if mill-workers' children were given state maintenance. It was this argument, that children must 'eat before they can learn',[52] which the S. D. F. and members of the Independent Labour Party took and used to reveal the exploitation of child labour, coupling their demand for abolition of the half-time system with proper welfare services to replace the earnings of child labour. Apart from the textile unions, they were supported by most groups in the labour movement, including the Trades Union Congress and the Workers' Educational Association as well as by a growing number of humanitarian reformers. They were all part of a wider movement which was concerned with all aspects of child welfare and which led, among other things, to the introduction of minimal welfare provisions by the Liberal governments after 1906, and was to lead eventually to the abolition of the half-time system in 1918 and its replacement with full-time education for all until the age of fourteen.

County Borough  of Bury.

Holt, Mayor.

# CONDITIONS

UPON WHICH

# CHILDREN are entitled to WORK HALF-TIME and FULL-TIME.

## HALF-TIME.

A Child of 12 YEARS OF AGE is entitled to a Certificate **TO WORK HALF-TIME:**

1,—If such child has attended **300 TIMES IN EACH YEAR** in not more than 2 Schools for 5 years, whether consecutive or not,

**OR**

2.—If such child has passed the 3rd STANDARD (Labour Examination) and would **IN THE OPINION OF THE COMMITTEE BE NECESSARILY AND BENEFICIALLY EMPLOYED.**

## FULL-TIME.

A child BETWEEN 13 AND 14 YEARS OF AGE is entitled to a Certificate **TO WORK FULL-TIME:**

1.—If such child has attended **350 TIMES IN EACH YEAR** in not more than 2 Schools for 5 years, whether consecutive or not,

**OR**

2.—If such child has passed the 5th STANDARD (Labour Examination).

**JOHN HASLAM,**

Corporation Offices, Bank Street, Bury,
31st December, 1900.

Clerk to the School
Attendance Committee.

Charles Vickerman & Sons, Printers, Bookbinders, &c., 19, Union Square, Bury.

## The end of half-time

The debates before the First World War suggest that there was a changing attitude in society toward half-time work. A change in perception had occurred between the legislation of 1844 when the half-timer was viewed as a worker gaining the benefits of part-time education, and the early twentieth-century perception of a schoolchild hampered by part-time work obligations. Notwithstanding the various arguments in favour of the half-time system which some textile workers continued to put, there is evidence that there was a widespread recognition of the inevitability of its demise. Improvements in the reliability of weaving technology, automatic doffing machines and the introduction of ring-spinning, albeit on a limited scale, were also beginning to undermine the demand for child labour. There is even reason to believe that it was becoming less popular in the textile districts because of the gradual improvement in the workers' living standards; this was certainly the argument, or the hope, expressed by some.[53]

In 1909 the InterDepartmental Committee on Partial Exemption from School Attendance recommended the ending of the system. In 1911 the Liberal government introduced a bill to abolish it, but it was not debated because of the pressure of other legislation; another bill in 1914 was successfully opposed by cotton manufacturing interests. But the writing was on the wall and by 1918 those who supported the half-time system were far outnumbered by those pressing for its abolition. The Education Act of that year abolished all partial and other exemptions, requiring all children to attend until they reached the school leaving age of fourteen years. To allow manufacturers to adjust, however, the half-time system was allowed to run down gradually over the next few years. Soon,

---

*Opposite*: A poster of 1900 produced by Bury's School Attendance Committee outlining the new regulations for exemption half-time at twelve and full-time at thirteen years of age which came into force after the passing of the Education Act in 1899. The emphasis on children being NECESSARILY AND BENE-FICIALLY EMPLOYED was deliberately intended to reduce the possibility of such exemptions. (Bury Metro, Reference and Information Services)

however, a feature which had been a part of growing up for many in cotton Lancashire had gone for ever.

## References

1. Oral History Collection; Centre for North West Regional Studies (CNWRS), Lancaster University, respondent Miss A.3.P., p. 6. (All interviews were conducted by Dr Elizabeth Roberts).
2. Oral History Collection, CNWRS, respondent Mr G.1.P., p. 88.
3. B. L. Hutchins and A. Harrison, *A History of Factory Legislation* (P. S. King, 1911), p. 85.
4. E. and R. Frow, *A Survey of the Half-Time System in Education* (Manchester, E. J. Morten, 1970), p. 17.
5. *The Schoolmaster*, 7 February 1885, p. 211.
6. H. Silver, 'Ideology and the Factory Child: Attitudes to Half-time Education', in P. McCann, (ed.), *Popular Education and Socialisation in the Nineteenth Century* (Methuen, 1977), pp. 141–66.
7. Quoted in A. H. Robson, *The Education of Children Employed in Industry, 1833–1876* (Kegan Paul, 1931), p. 96.
8. PP, 1862, xxii, p. 255.
9. M. Cruickshank, *Children and Industry: Child Health and Welfare in North-West Textile Towns during the Nineteenth Century* (Manchester University Press, 1981), pp. 95–6; Frow, *The Half-Time System*, p. 51.
10. S. J. Chapman, *The Lancashire Cotton Industry: a Study in Economic Development* (Manchester University Press, 1904), p. 112.
11. D. A. Farnie, *The English Cotton Industry and the World Market, 1815–1896* (Oxford, Clarendon Press, 1979), p. 301.
12. Accrington Borough Council Education Committee Quarterly Reports 1903–1916, LRO.
13. H. Catling, *The Spinning Mule* (David and Charles, 1970, repr. Lancashire County Council, 1986) pp. 170–73.
14. Museums at Higher Mill Museum, Helmshore and Quarry Bank Mill, Styal have regular demonstrations of this and other processes.
15. Catling, *The Spinning Mule*, p. 156.
16. ibid., p. 177.
17. ibid., p. 173.
18. Frow, *The Half-Time System*, p. 58; B. Simon, *Education and the Labour Movement 1870–1920* (Lawrence and Wishart, 1974), p. 140.
19. J. R. Clynes, *Memoirs 1869–1924* (1937), p. 29.
20. Catling, *The Spinning Mule*, pp. 171–79.
21. Simon, *Education and the Labour Movement*, p. 138.
22. Verbal recollection of Mrs Phyllis Rutter collected by the authors.
23. Oral History Collection, CNWRS, respondent Mrs O.1.P., p. 2.

24. ibid., respondent Mr G.1.P., p. 2.
25. ibid., respondent Mrs O.1.P., p. 19.
26. ibid., respondent Mr P.2.P., pp. 6–7.
27. *Report of the Inter-Departmental Committee on Partial Exemption from School Attendance*, Appendix 11, PP, 1909, xvii, pp. 1018–23.
28. Simon, *Education and the Labour Movement*, p. 139.
29. *Cotton Factory Times*, 30 June 1899.
30. *Cotton Factory Times*, 20 January 1899.
31. *Cotton Factory Times*, 2 June 1899.
32. *Cotton Factory Times*, 24 March 1899.
33. *Cotton Factory Times*, 20 January 1899.
34. *Cotton Factory Times*, 24 March 1899.
35. *Cotton Factory Times*, 27 January 1899.
36. *Cotton Factory Times*, 10 February 1899.
37. *Cotton Factory Times*, 17 February 1899.
38. Quoted in L. Rose, *The Erosion of Childhood: Child Oppression in Britain, 1860–1918* (Routledge, 1991), p. 115.
39. Frow, *The Half-Time System*, p. 25.
40. *The Schoolmaster*, 27 December 1884.
41. B. Webb, *The Case for the Factory Acts*, (1901) p. 134.
42. Rose, *The Erosion of Childhood*, p. 148. The payment by results system was phased out after 1890.
43. Accrington Wesleyan Day Schools Log Book 1863–1905. 16 January 1869, LRO.
44. Oral History Collection, CNWRS, respondent Mr F.1.P., p. 31.
45. ibid., respondent Mr G.1.P., p. 2.
46. Frow, *The Half-Time System*, p. 19; Webb, *The Case for the Factory Acts*, p. 111.
47. Oral History Collection, CNWRS, respondent Mr F.1.P. p. 98.
48. *The Schoolmaster*, 27 December 1884.
49. Webb, *The Case for the Factory Acts*, p. 98.
50. Clynes, *Memoirs*, pp. 29–30.
51. Allen Clarke, *The Effects of the Factory System* (London, Grant Richards, 1899; repr. Littleborough, George Kelsall, 1989), pp. 96–101.
52. Simon, *Education and the Labour Movement*, p. 141.
53. Frow, *The Half-Time System*, p. 59.

Chapter 4

# Children and young people on the land

*Simone Coombs and Deborah Radburn*

*The image of Lancashire handed down by generations of economics textbooks is one of the classic case of industrialisation. The mental landscape is composed of red brick terraces, cotton mills and coal mines. There is little place for agriculture. Yet Lancashire was, at the same time as being the industrial heartland of the Empire, an agricultural county of importance.[1]*

IMAGES of mill and mine have dominated the landscape of Lancashire, most memorably in mid-Victorian fiction, from Charles Dickens' *Hard Times* to the novels of Elizabeth Gaskell such as *Mary Barton* and *North and South*. They have also been the focus for investigations into child labour in the county since the early nineteenth century, a concern evident in numerous government reports and popular tracts of the period. In contrast, very little was written about *agricultural* Lancashire or the position of its workers in the nineteenth century. Although the competition held by the Royal Agricultural Society in 1849 produced a number of reports on the county, these, in comparison to the prolific and dramatic portrayals of industrial Lancashire, suggest that the agricultural labour of children was not perceived as a pressing or wide-ranging problem in this period.

Furthermore, Lancashire's dominant manufacturing became, and has remained, symbolic of an 'industrial north', to be contrasted with depictions of a 'rural south'. This geographical division of industry and agriculture has meant that any attention given to rural areas has tended to focus upon the south of England where there was concern expressed about agricultural distress, unrest and depression. Studies of child labour in the nineteenth century reflect this, dividing the country into the experiences of northern industry and southern agriculture, and thus overlook the experience of child labour in the rural districts of Lancashire.[2]

Boy labour in nineteenth-century agriculture has been typically described as a chronology of scaring off birds, tending animals, driving the plough and assisting of the carter or cowman, with a gradual integration into waged work, ending in full-time employment as a day labourer or a hired servant, most commonly between the ages of twelve and fourteen. Girls however, did not begin work in the fields, but within the home, often before taking up employment in service as dairymaids or household servants, whilst both boys and girls were often called upon to help both at home and in the fields at hay time and harvest.

The children of rural Lancashire shared some of these experiences; the nature of their work reflected their age and gender, and was often governed by the calendar in arable areas, where the demand for extra labour was predominantly seasonal. But patterns of child labour were dependent on the type of local farming and role of the family within the agricultural community and this is where much of Lancashire's agricultural work differed from that depicted in the accepted view of child labour in rural England.

The little boy scaring crows in a field of waving corn is not a scene which is recorded in any local sources for this period; arable farming, primarily in south-west Lancashire and on the Fylde, was more concerned with root crops and vegetables. Binns observed some examples of this trade as early as 1851, noting that 'many acres of onions are grown' around Ormskirk and Rufford while towards Southport 'all the carrots are produced for Liverpool and some other markets: Saturday is chief market day, when 1500 or 2000 carts laden with hay, straw, potatoes, turnips, onions and other vegetables, with milk and butter pass through the toll gate'.[3] Lancashire, however, was primarily a pastoral county and became more so over the century with dairying and stock rearing and, in the upland fells, sheep dominating the local economy. Except on some farms in the low lying lands to the west which were suitable for labour-intensive cultivation, the county's system of farming differed from the national

Fruit picking at Tarleton, *c.* 1908. The rich soil of south-west Lancashire was suited to intensive fruit and vegetable cultivation. Soft fruit accounted for a tiny percentage of crops but its importance was increasing in the decades before the First World War. (Lancashire County Library, Tarleton Local Studies Collection)

picture of large farms employing gangs of labourers; it was dominated by relatively small family-run farms. All the commentators throughout the century remarked on this and it is supported by official statistics. According to the census of 1851, three-quarters of Lancashire farms occupied fewer than fifty acres each, and the agricultural returns after 1870 show that little changed into the twentieth century; Lancashire had the lowest average farm size (40 acres) in the country.[4] Any survey of the county, therefore, must begin first with these family-run farms.

## *Family farms*

Small farmers employed very few servants and only limited seasonal agricultural labour when necessary. Beesley wrote in 1849, 'Excepting during harvest a great number of the smaller farmers employ no day labourers and many no farm servants, the work of the farm being done by the farmer and his family'.[5] This view is supported by the claims of the farmers. In 1894, Mr Dobson, a farmer of fifty seven and a half acres in the Garstang area, reported, 'I and my wife and two daughters work the farm and we employ extra labour at hay time'.[6] For small farmers it was often women and children who effectively ran the farm. Wilson Fox described several instances of this in his report to the Royal Commission on Agriculture in 1894. Around Hambleton small farmers

> risen from the ranks of labourers, had to look to other means of money-making besides their holdings. Thus some are hucksters, some get employment in works, or some as labourers on farms . . . one man on twenty six acres of grassland kept cows and sheep and was employed on a farm as day labour, his wife and family looking after the stock in his absence.

Labourers on Fitzherbert Brockhole's estate at Claughton who rented smallholdings 'sell butter in Preston and Garstang', and their 'wives and children do the necessary work'.[7]

This situation obviously had an important impact on the demand for child labour. Younger children were often to be found working for their parents in and around the farm, creating an invisible labour force which was often overlooked in official sources. The census for 1851, for example, did not acknowledge that young children would be working on family farms; 'those under fifteen are returned as children simply or scholars'.[8] Much of the heavier work on farms was undoubtedly carried out by children in their teens, and it is likely that young children were only engaged in menial work, but children as young as twelve could be employed full-time. Significant numbers of 10–14 year-olds are recorded in the census of 1871 under the category of 'farmers' relatives', who were regarded as 'usually engaged in the business of the farm', and young people between fifteen and nineteen who worked for their families constituted 36 per cent of males employed in agriculture in that age group, and 73 per cent of females.[9]

The work which farmers' relatives did, far from being easier, was often more arduous than those employed from outside the family. This was especially so in times of agricultural crisis, as in the mid-1890s. Wilson Fox observed

> In many cases where the employment of less outdoor labour has been a necessity the land has not suffered because the farmer and his sons have increased exertion, and if an indoor servant has had to be sent away, the wife and daughters have undertaken additional dairy work and household duties. Thus at the present time in some districts it is the farmers' sons and daughters who have suffered rather than the land.[10]

Despite the obvious hard work involved in this kind of labour, evidence suggests that, although they were employed full-time, children and young relatives were often not given a wage. A footnote to Wilson Fox's report on Garstang in 1894 explained that 'A few farmers told me that they give their sons and daughters wages, but this is quite the exception, and I believe, in the great majority of cases they are simply working for their food and clothes'. In the same report he documents the case of the son of a farmer who, on wanting to get married, asked his parents for money; they declined, as they had none saved. His fiancée, however, having been engaged in domestic service, produced her savings of £200. The great differences in their financial situations led the son, now a farmer in his own right to demand that 'Every farmer should put his children's wages by or else give up the farm. I have to pay for labour, and others ought to do so, and not let their children suffer'.[11] It is unlikely that this wish would have been fulfilled, the attraction of free labour in return for subsistence being an obvious inducement to use the family on the farm, especially in times of depression.

Much of the work children and young people did on Lancashire farms was, however, similar to that of other rural areas, in that it was determined by age and gender. Work for the very young and for older girls was centred around household chores and simple tasks around the farm, while boys were more likely to be employed in outdoor work. The increasing market for meat and dairy products throughout the century, stimulated by urban population growth and prosperity and by better transport links, enabled Lancashire farmers to supply the industrial centres with perishable produce. Many of the references to child labour on small farms, therefore, highlight the importance attached to dairying. This was traditionally connected with the domestic sphere, much of the butter- and cheese-making taking place in the farm kitchen, so it was considered to be female work. Girls, therefore, were more likely to help their mothers in the dairy, whilst their brothers would help their fathers, by attending to the animals or a small plot of land. In 1849 Beesley acknowledged that 'The wife or daughter of the farmer is generally a dairymaid'.[12] Reverend W. Stratton, vicar at Gressingham in the Lune valley, reported to the Royal Commission on the Employment of Women and Children in Agriculture in 1868–9 that 'In my parish most of the young children (that is under thirteen), are employed at home looking after the garden and cows of their parents, and thus are getting some practical training without hard labour'.[13] This observation suggests that farm work carried out in or near the home, far from being arduous, was seen as beneficial to the child. As children got older and attended school, they were expected to help out morning and evening while 'farmers' boys and girls living within two or three miles of a large town often have a large milk round to go over'.[14]

In south-west Lancashire, where arable produce was likely to be sold at market, or elsewhere where farmers also grew root crops, much more intense labour was required at certain times of the year. A consequence of this for the small farmer was that he was forced to rely upon the labour of his children, especially when he could not afford, or acquire, adult labourers. The extra labour undertaken by the children of small farmers who grew vegetable crops for market is described by Binns in his 1851 report, *Notes on the Agriculture of Lancashire*. His example is not drawn from the area around Liverpool, however, where arable farming and market-gardening were most extensively practised, but from Poulton-le-Sands. Here the land was also suitable for growing vegetables, and the prosperity of the small farms depended on crops being sold in the markets at Preston, Manchester, Carlisle, Kendal and parts of Yorkshire. He mentions the fishermen-farmers, observing that 'The fishing season ends towards the latter end of May, and gives them leisure to attend their agricultural pursuits, in which they are very skilful and industrious'. These fishermen-farmers and the other local farmers are recorded as employing the labour of their children on the land. 'When the season of planting arrives, which, if the weather be favourable is about the last week in March, the seed mostly of ash-leaved kidney, is put in drills of two feet apart; but the lazy bed way is mostly adopted by smallholders. A man with a couple of women and boys will plant a quarter of an acre in a day.' Onions were also grown using their labour; '. . . the sowing commences on the first or second week in March . . . The weeding is all performed by women and children, who may be seen at work day after day, on a small extent of ground'.[15] As with dairying, urban growth and better rail transport increased the demand for the produce of these small farms.

As well as working on the farm, there were other jobs a rural child could undertake which were centred around the home and which helped to boost family income. These varied over the county and changed during the century. Handloom weaving was widely reported to the Poor Law Commission in the early 1830s as an occupation which employed children in rural districts, while children in West Derby, in the south west of the county, obtained employment 'picking bristles for brush manufac-turers'.[16] Localised cottage industries continued to use their labour later in the century. Another example appears in the Burscough school log book, in an entry for March 1875: 'Several children are away this week working for the basket makers and in the gardens'.[17] The Reverend E. F. Manby, rector of Poulton-le-Sands, described another job in the evidence collected for the 1868–9 Commission. 'Many much younger children here are employed for the greater part of the day in picking shrimps. You may see in many houses mere infants seated at a table thus employed for hours together. The shrimps are prepared for potting or tea parties, and children four years old can earn in this way 6d or 9d a day.'[18]

This localised, home-centred labour did not attract extensive national attention or governmental concern, despite being hard work and often entailing long hours. Only with regard to the neglect of education for younger children was it really decried. Clergymen were particularly critical of this in their reports to the Royal Commission on the Employment of Women and Children in the late 1860s. Mr Powis, rector of Farrington, was generally pleased with the level of education in his parish, but commented that 'It is only where small farms prevail that the education of children is materially interrupted'. Canon Hubbersty of Cartmel also bemoaned 'the practice of small farmers in withdrawing their children from school at too early an age, and the result is that in a year or two they lose almost all that they had acquired'. Henry Tremenheere, reporting generally on the situation in north Lancashire at the time, argued that 'the attendance of the children of agricultural labourers is much more regular, and extends over a larger period of the year than of small farmers'.[19] James Bryce, Assistant Commissioner for the School Inquiry Commission, provided a vivid description of what he suggested was a typical upbringing for the son of a small farmer in the county in the 1860s.

The farmer's or labourer's child (for it matters little which we take) learns his letters at home, goes to school at nine, and plods away at reading and spelling for a year or two, usually under the charge (in a Privy Council School) of some pupil teacher or (in an Endowed School) of an incompetent assistant. At eleven his hand is just beginning to have some power over the pen and his mind to have some faint comprehension of arithmetical processes. But at eleven he is also beginning to be of use in the fields. He is kept away all the time of the hay harvest and corn harvest, and of the potato picking which follows. If he lives on moory ground, like that of the upper reaches of the Lune and Wyre, or along the banks of the Ribble estuary, he is taken off to help in the turf-cutting; if near the coast he is sent out to gather shrimps and cockles. Thus attending school only some five or six months in the year, he is unable to make real progress in arithmetic, much less in geography and grammar; and when he is finally removed from school at thirteen, he has not grown familiar enough with the use of the pen to write his name in the marriage register ten years afterwards, nor fluent enough in reading to care if he ever opens a book again.[20]

Even after schooling had been made compulsory, farmers' children were often taken out of school to work and school authorities were sometimes obliged to threaten their parents with the law, as at Hambleton in the early 1880s, when several farmers were called before the school board for illegally employing their children.[21] The problems of administration and the reluctance of local school boards to prosecute, however, meant that legal action was rare. Even so, all these observations strengthen the view that the small farmer depended on family labour to supplement and maintain household income on a permanent basis throughout the period.

## *The seasonal labour force*

Although family labour was important on the pastoral farms for much of the year, seasonal employment patterns were more akin to the national picture, with many more children of other families likely to be involved in work away from the home. Unlike most of the country, however, the harvesting of cereal crops was not the busiest time of the year, although this did require more labour. More important were hay, grown as vital animal feed and harvested between late June and September, and potatoes gathered later in the autumn. Away from the coalfields, peat cutting was also an important occupation for labouring families, largely for winter fuel. Binns commented that in 'low Furness . . . the labourer has also the advantage of the employment of cutting peat, for fuel, at three shillings per day, often taking two of his children, who have for spreading the peats, 10*d*. to one shilling per day each, he also has harvest wages and mowing wages'.[22] The practice was similar in areas of the Fylde like Pilling where 'boys are required chiefly for planting and gathering potatoes and in wheeling turfs to the carts for stacking. The moss provides most of the fuel of the district'.[23] Even in the 1890s Wilson Fox noted that every cottage had its peat stack. Neither this, nor potato lifting, was carried out by the gang labour evident in places like the Fens, since the father of a family usually took his children, with one or two of his neighbours, to assist in such work.

Some of this seasonal demand for harvest labour was often met by non-agricultural workers. Up to the middle of the century, weavers were frequently employed, Beesley noting in 1849 that 'The numerous hand loom weavers resident in the agricultural districts vacate the loom for the spade and sickle during the summer season, in potato planting and "getting up" hay making and reaping, but return to the loom in winter, when the demand for their labour ceases'.[24] It was not only males, however, who were employed; the evidence provided by the parish overseer for Kirkham to the 1834 Poor Law Commission observed that 'in the harvest months women and children, who are of sufficient age are employed in reaping, at other times in weaving'.[25]

Binns sheds some light on some of the roles of the young workers in the hay harvest. 'As soon as the grass is cut, women and children are employed

Hay making at Dixon's farm, Foulridge. Although clearly posed, and with the church in the background to add to an image of rural tranquillity, this photograph is nevertheless a reminder that farming remained an important activity even in industrial east Lancashire. The dense population settlements were surrounded by relatively small farms which largely specialised in dairying. (Lancashire County Library, Colne Local Studies Collection)

to spread it abroad with their hands, this they do with great dexterity, taking care that the grass is perfectly separate, that is, that no tufts or "sops" be left.'[26] After this the hay was raked, gathered into cocks, then stacked in the barn. It was often a lengthy process, which is the reason why many school holidays were often extended or begun earlier to correspond with the mowing. The extent of this seasonal child labour in agricultural families is perhaps best documented from the absenteeism and school holiday periods in the rural school log books. Brathay District School at Skelwith in the largely pastoral area of High Furness, is an excellent example.

*1886*
*9 August:* In consequence of the backward state of the hay harvest the school holidays have been prolonged to the 14th.
*16 August:* Commenced a week today. The attendance is still poor.
*20 August:* The attendance has been poor during the week but several children are still engaged in the hay fields.

*1887*
*14 June:* Average very low owing partly to the commencement of hay time. Advised the managers to allow the holiday to begin at once and continue for five weeks.[27]

The Clitheroe Union Attendance Committee minutes for June 1879–81 give another example of the way in which school terms were interrupted for seasonal labour. The committee repeatedly

resolved that the authority exempt from the prohibitions and restrictions of the Elementary Education Acts the employment of children above the age of eight years for the necessary operations of husbandry and the ingathering of crops for the period of five weeks from the fourth of July next and the clerk is instructed to issue notice accordingly, but not to advertise the same in any newspaper.[28]

Child seasonal labour in many parts of Lancashire, especially in the south-west and the Fylde, was dominated by the potato crop. Potatoes had long been important in Lancashire agriculture. In 1815 Dickson wrote that 'There is perhaps no county in the kingdom, where more attention is bestowed in cultivating this useful root, than in this, as it was probably the first to which its culture was introduced'.[29] Land drainage and reclamation throughout the century, especially on the coastal moss lands, led to an increase of arable land in this area and in the Fylde and to an extension of potato cultivation. In 1905 Lancashire's potato output amounted to 413,871 tons, which constituted 15.8 per cent of the national production.[30]

Potato digging at Tarleton. Potatoes accounted for around twenty per cent of farm acreage in Lancashire and were an integral part of the county's diet. A growing scarcity of casual male labour for digging resulted in rising wage rates during the 1890s and encouraged larger farmers to adopt new technology. Women and children were still employed to pick up after the digger. (Lancashire County Library, Tarleton Local Studies Collection)

The child's role in the growing of this crop was, therefore, inevitably going to be important. Dickson had noted that during the potato planting season 'women and children are often employed in dropping the sets into the furrows or drills'. The method involved used 'the dibble or setting stick', which was 'employed by one person who makes the holes into which the sets are dropped', and, he explained, 'children can perform this work very well'. This method of potato planting was dominant early in the century. Children were also extensively employed in the potato harvest. As the market expanded larger farms began to adopt mechanical aids. The rise of mechanisation in south-west Lancashire has been documented by Alistair Mutch using information in notices of farm sales in the local

Young potato pickers near Chorley. Potato picking provided considerable employment for whole communities. School holidays were scheduled to coincide with the busiest periods and farmers sought to emphasise that children's involvement was positively beneficial to their welfare. 'As a rule they seem to enjoy it and seem proud that they are earning a little money and assisting their parents . . . it helps to make them more active, energetic and industrious in their later lives,' insisted a Mr Mercer of Prescot in his evidence to the government inquiry into the employment of school children in 1902. (Lancashire County Library, Chorley Local Studies Collection)

newspapers. He showed that machines, like the mechanised potato digger, far from leading to a decline in employment, could actually increase demand for child and female labour. Mutch suggested that 'once a digger was used, considerable savings on labour could be made, since adult males

84

previously employed for turning the soil were replaced by the digger'. The type of labour required in gathering the potatoes, however, was 'qualitatively different and could be done by either women or children', who could be employed as potato pickers at 'two shillings a day', which was 'less than a man on piece-work'. He also notes that 'schoolchildren were cheaper and faster than adults and their availability stimulated the demand for diggers'.[31] It seems then that agricultural machinery and child labour were complementary; the availability of young workers could even stimulate the use of machines in agriculture, and vice versa.

As in their recording of other seasonal occupations, the census returns do not reflect this temporary demand for child labour at the potato harvest. However, once again the school log books furnish us with adequate evidence of the extent to which children were used. The springtime absences mainly span the period of late March to mid-April, when children could be employed in planting, weeding, hoeing or the spreading of manure. The dominant references, however, are to the harvest periods which fell directly within the autumn term. The Burscough school log book for 12 October 1874 reads: 'Very thin school only forty eight present in the morning. I do not know the cause, except that it is potato time'.[32] As at hay-time and summer harvest, the school holidays were often manipulated to suit patterns of agricultural demand so as to prevent absenteeism. In Aughton in 1898, for example, a school holiday was scheduled to coincide with the potato lifting in October. The labour of schoolchildren during the late autumn 'lifting' and for harvesting of other market-garden crops remained in demand in the Ormskirk areas and on the Fylde well into the twentieth century.

Seasonal labour, therefore, whether at hay-time or potato harvesting, often seemed either to employ direct child labour, or to be the cause of a child remaining at home to care for infants while other members of the family worked in the fields. As these references show, educational legislation on agricultural child labour existed by the end of the nineteenth century. This was designed to prevent exploitation, but without interrupting or inconveniencing farmers. Restrictions were predominantly connected with school attendance. The 1867 Agricultural Gangs Act had little relevance for Lancashire's rural areas since, as we have seen, no gangs were employed. Various Education Acts after 1870 which endeavoured to extend compulsory education were more important but these still made allowance for farm work. The Agricultural Children's Act of 1873, which sought to secure a minimum attendance for 8–12 year-olds, could be undermined by farmers' appeals to local petty sessions, and any child living more than two miles from school was also not obliged to attend. Subsequent Acts enforced compulsory attendance but still gave local school boards and attendance committees the power to allow children who had made a certain number of attendances, or had reached the specified standard of academic achievement, to be released earlier than the normal school-leaving age. Schools also had the freedom to adapt to local needs, as the Clitheroe and Ormskirk examples show, by extending or creating a holiday to coincide with busy agricultural periods. Legislation, therefore, may have created a legal and social divide between young children and full-time workers but it had little effect on seasonal labour.

## Farm servants

Farmers throughout Lancashire regularly complained that they were unable to obtain sufficient adult male and female labour. The reasons for this were various: alternative regional employment, such as in the mills, mines and iron works; the emphasis on family-based labour; and the increasing migration of teenagers and young adults into the towns. Unable to find sufficient workers willing to work for weekly wages, farmers continued the practice of farm service, where workers were hired for six or twelve months and boarded with the family. Small farmers might employ a lad or a girl to assist until their own children were old enough to help on the farm, but the main employers of full-time labour were the larger mixed stock and arable farmers who needed a permanent labour force to attend to animal husbandry and heavy seasonal work.

On leaving school, children in the northern part of the county would usually have been engaged on a six-monthly basis at Whitsuntide or Martinmas, being put out to service either by their parents or hired at the fairs at Kendal, Lancaster and Ulverston.[33] This type of employment was especially attractive to poorer families as it provided accommodation and board at a time when family size was often very large, and cottage

86

accommodation limited and poor. In Dalton in 1834 it was reported that 'Children at fourteen and eleven are sent to service by the parents, or the parish ballots them apprentices in husbandry'.[34] Further south, in the Fylde, servants were usually engaged each February for a year. The census returns for 1851 and 1871, analysed by Mutch, are useful for revealing the preponderance of such 'live-in' servants in Lancashire's rural work-force.[35] Agricultural labourers only accounted for a minority of the labour force and were more concentrated in the south-west of the county in the arable districts. In contrast, live-in, hired servants were the norm elsewhere in the county. In Cartmel, for example, there was a dramatic drop in the number of labourers between 1851 and 1871 but a rise in the number of farm servants. Mutch suggests that this reflected changes from an arable to a predominantly pastoral economy in the district, but it may also be due to the difficulty of getting young men to work unless they were given longer-term contracts.[36] Females were more likely to be returned as domestic servants rather than farm labourers in the census, and Reverend W. Stratton, vicar of Gressingham, noted that 'In the Vale of the Lune it is the exception to find women and girls employed in outdoor work: there is a great demand for them as house and farm servants and wages are higher'.[37]

Unfortunately contemporary sources do not provide extensive information on how these young servants were occupied. Some of the work which female servants did undoubtedly involved farm work, especially in the dairy where they were expected to help with butter- and cheese-making. In arable farming, lads were often employed as ploughboys, especially on the heavy lands. In 1815 Dickson acknowledged that 'where three horse teams were in use a boy was employed to drive them',[38] whilst the 1868 Commission received a report from Jonathan Butler, a land agent from Poulton-le-Fylde, who acknowledged that 'Ploughboys were used . . . usually 12 year-old boys are competent enough'. Another large farmer from the same area, however, suggested that such young boys were only capable of doing 'odd jobs . . . but we are obliged to get them young, or we should not get them at all'.[39] Some farmers by this time were claiming that they felt an increased urgency to employ children at a younger age. 'I found twelve a common age at which children are first engaged as farm servants . . . to secure labourers as young as possible and thus prevent their being attracted to the towns which in this county, compete in the labour market so successfully with the country.'[40] This practice of hiring boys as young as twelve led to similar criticisms to those made about sons of small farmers being taken out of school, but others stressed that it was a beneficial system since the control was good for them, and they were under a stricter discipline than at home.

## *'Cockling'*

One unusual example of child labour, however, which was universally condemned by farmers, clergymen and government commissioners, was the coastal employment in 'cockling'.

As early as 1834 information gathered as part of the Poor Law Commission's enquiry briefly mentioned 'gathering cockles on the sand' at Bolton-le-Sands.[41] The 1868–9 Commission provides more valuable

Cocklers at Silverdale in the late nineteenth century. Both local farmers and clergymen condemned the involvement of young children in this trade in the late 1860s. 'Cockling children must begin early', observed a Mr Burrow of Flookburgh, 'little things of five years old go out to help a little and to learn.' (Lancaster City Council, Museums Service)

information not only of the practice but also of local opinions on the matter. Henry Tremenheere reported that 'great numbers of children, young persons and women who reside in the small villages on the coast of Morecambe Bay go upon the sands on every recession of the tide in parties of from ten to twenty and pursue their occupation until the advancing tide compels them to return'. He considered that around 300 children were involved and explained that, weather permitting, it was an all-year-round occupation, the cockles being packed and sent off to markets in the manufacturing towns to the south.

Farmers complained that this employment robbed them of local labour and pushed up wages, but the local clergy's concerns about this form of work are typical of those expressed about other child labour in the

Shrimping was a major occupation at Morecambe well into the twentieth century. Women and girls were employed to pick or shell the shrimps and to bag them for sale. Such work was largely carried out indoors and attracted less criticism than cockling. (Lancaster City Council, Museums Service)

nineteenth century, not only in connection with the child's health, in that 'the stooping posture is bad', but more importantly in the effects which it had on their education and morals. 'Owing to the value of their labour to their parents and the early age of which it is made available (from five years of age), cocklers are never sent to school, and grow up in a state of absolute ignorance, and I fear I must add of heathenism.' The Reverend Mr Rigg of Hawkshead complained that they have not 'the slightest education' and 'they never enter a place of worship', thus the money they earned was 'at the expense of their intellectual and moral debasement'.[42] 'Cockling' could, it seems, provide a substantial addition to the family's income and it was, as the Commission noted, too attractive for parents to ignore, but, unlike other forms of agricultural work, it was not one which met with their approval, being the only mode of employment which was considered similar to the gang labour force in the south and east of England.

## Conclusion

As we have seen, the needs of the rural family meant that child labour was inevitable, whether at home on the farm, seasonally in the harvest, or through full-time employment at a slightly older age. But child labour in Lancashire, apart from cockling, was not perceived as especially physically or morally wrong; it was considered unavoidable, as is shown in the practice of changing the school holiday periods. Children usually worked with their families and rarely in agricultural 'gangs' and so failed to attract the attention and criticism which such gangs did further south. This lack of concern is reflected in the comparative lack of historical sources on Lancashire's rural child labour and is the main reason why it is difficult to document the subject. Indeed, no information on the county was collected for the 1843 Poor Law Enquiry into the Employment of Women and Children in Agriculture. Lancashire's rural child labour was largely invisible and was not perceived as a problem because it was family-based or connected with farm service. These aspects perhaps removed perceptions of child exploitation, but they did not mean that child labour was irrelevant to the agricultural economy, or that it was any less vital to its success.

# References

1. A. Mutch, 'Rural Society in Lancashire 1840–1914' (unpublished Ph.D. thesis, University of Manchester, 1980), p. 19.
2. P. Horn, *The Victorian Country Child* (Stroud, Alan Sutton, 1985) chapter 5 on work contains no references to Lancashire.
3. J. Binns, *Notes on the Agriculture of Lancashire* (Preston, 1851), p. 141.
4. *Census of Great Britain, 1851*, Division VIII, North West Counties, p. 658; J. K. Walton, *Lancashire: a social history 1558–1939* (Manchester University Press, 1987), p. 122; *Agriculture Returns of Great Britain for 1895*, PP, 1896, lxvii, Tables IX and X.
5. G. Beesley, *A Report on the State of Agriculture in Lancashire* (Preston, 1849), p. 28.
6. *Royal Commission on Agriculture*, PP, 1894, xvi., Evidence attached to report by Mr Wilson Fox on the Garstang Union, p. 63.
7. *Royal Commission on Agriculture*, PP, 1894, xvi, Report on Garstang Union, p. 16.
8. *Census of Great Britain, 1851*, Occupations, Table 34 explanatory note.
9. *Census, 1871*; Occupations of the Population, Division VIII, North Western Counties, Table 11.
10. *Royal Commission on Agriculture*, PP, 1894, xvi, Report on Garstang Union, p. 14.
11. ibid.
12. Beesley, *State of Agriculture in Lancashire*, p. 27.
13. *Royal Commission on the Employment of Women and Children in Agriculture*, PP, 1868–9, xiii, Evidence attached to report by Assistant Commissioner, J. Henry Tremenheere on North Lancashire, p. 563.
14. *Inter-Departmental Committee on the Employment of School Children*, PP, 1902, xxv, Appendix 2, Replies from country correspondents (W. Bainbridge, Secretary of the Lancaster Agricultural Society).
15. Binns, *Agriculture of Lancashire*, p. 105.
16. *Royal Commission on the Poor Law*, PP, 1834, xxx, Answers to Rural Queries Part I, questions 11–13, pp. 277–86.
17. St. John's Church of England School, Burscough Bridge, log book, 12 March 1875, LRO, SMBu/1/1.
18. *Royal Commission on the Employment of Women and Children in Agriculture*, PP, 1868–9, xiii, Evidence accompanying report on North Lancashire, p. 560.
19. *Royal Commission on the Employment of Women and Children in Agriculture*, PP, 1868–9, xiii, Report on North Lancashire, p. 63
20. *Schools Inquiry Commission*, 1868, ix, General Reports of the Assistant Commissioners; Report of Mr J. Bryce on Lancashire, p. 702.
21. Hambleton School Board Minute Book, 10 May 1882, LRO, SBH/1.
22. Binns, *Agriculture of Lancashire*, p. 105.
23. *Royal Commission on the Employment of Women and Children in Agriculture*, PP, 1868–9, xiii, Evidence of Revd J. D. Bannister, Rector of Pilling, p. 561.
24. Beesley, *State of Agriculture in Lancashire*, p. 28.
25. *Royal Commission on the Poor Law*, PP, 1834, xxx, Answers to Rural Queries, p. 282.

26. Binns, *Agriculture of Lancashire*, p. 88.
27. Brathay District School, Skelwith, log book, Autumn Term 1886 and June 1887, LRO, SMSK/1/1.
28. Clitheroe Union School Attendance Committee Minutes, 27 June 1881, LRO PUC/8/1.
29. R. W. Dickson, *General View of the Agriculture of Lancashire*, (London, 1815), pp. 365–6.
30. Mutch, 'Rural Society in Lancashire 1840–1914', p. 19.
31. ibid., p. 80.
32. Burscough Bridge School log book, LRO, SMBu/1/1.
33. Mutch, 'Rural Society in Lancashire 1840–1914', p. 183.
34. *Royal Commission on the Poor Law*, PP, 1834, xxx, Answers to Rural Queries, pp. 279, 281.
35. 'Farm servants' were no longer separately listed after 1871 so it is not possible to distinguish them in the census from agricultural labourers who were hired by the day or week.
36. Mutch, 'Rural Society in Lancashire 1840–1914', pp. 171–3.
37. *Royal Commission on the Employment of Women and Children in Agriculture*, PP, 1868–9, xiii, Evidence attached to report on North Lancashire, p. 563.
38. Dickson, *General View of the Agriculture of Lancashire*, p. 236.
39. *Royal Commission on the Employment of Women and Children in Agriculture*, PP, 1868–9, xiii, Evidence attached to report on North Lancashire, p. 561–2.
40. *Royal Commission on the employment of Women and Children in Agriculture*, PP, 1868–9, xiii, Report by J. H. Tremenheere, p. 155.
41. *Royal Commission on the Poor Law*, PP, 1834, xxx, Answers to Rural Queries, p. 277.
42. *Royal Commission on the Employment of Women and Children in Agriculture*, PP, 1868–9, xiii, Report by J. H. Tremenheere, p. 156.

Chapter 5

# The 'Boy Labour Problem' in Lancashire

*Barbara Copeland and Gavin Thompson*

ONCERN about children's employment in a variety of industrial occupations led to the passage of a series of Factory Acts throughout the
nineteenth century. At the end of the century and into the 1900s, however,
attention shifted to different jobs which had developed largely in response
to the growth of services, and to slightly older children. In particular, too
many boys, from the age of about ten to the mid-teens, were thought to be
taking up unskilled work which gave them an uncertain long-term future
in the labour market, while also harming them physically and morally.

During the second half of the nineteenth century there were considerable changes in the distribution of the national labour force. 'In terms of
employment, services comprised 31.3 per cent of the total in 1861, and
grew both in absolute and relative terms to account for 41.4 per cent of all
employment in 1911.'[1] These included transport, distribution, banking and
commerce, the professions and government services which developed in
the wake of industrialisation and urbanisation. A further development was
the emergence of the mass market, stimulated by the growth of population,
which rose from twenty-seven million in 1851 to forty-five million in 1911,
and by an increase in spending power as real wages improved from the
mid 1870s. Greater prosperity, together with a reduction in working hours,
also led to increased leisure activities and the growth of the seaside holiday
industry which needed unskilled, seasonal workers who were predominantly young.

The distribution of occupations taken up by boys depended on the
economy of their local area. In Lancashire the most noticeable growth in

93

the service sector was centred on the large commercial cities of Liverpool and Manchester and the county's expanding seaside resorts, such as Blackpool, Southport and Morecambe, rather than in the industrial and manufacturing towns. A national enquiry in 1893–4 examined the different types of employment which boys went into after leaving school.[2] It is very noticeable from this that Liverpool and Manchester had the highest numbers and proportions of boys entering clerical work and transport sectors in Lancashire. These two categories together employed 53 per cent of boys leaving school in each of the above cities, whereas Oldham and Blackburn show only 7–9 per cent and Preston and Rochdale 15 per cent entering these trades. The percentages were slightly higher for the industrial towns of St Helens/Widnes and Barrow, with 18 and 19 respectively. The figures also show differences in patterns of shopwork, though these are not as striking, with Manchester and Liverpool still having larger percentage of boys entering retailing than the textile, chemical or shipbuilding towns.

It is clear, then, that the well-established manufacturing economies of the textile towns were able to provide more regular, industrial work for the majority of school-leavers. The 1911 census gives further proof of this, showing that 70–80 per cent of boys aged as young as thirteen years were already at work full-time in the textile towns, whereas only 5 and 13 per cent of boys of the same age were employed in Liverpool and Manchester respectively. Over half of the fourteen year-olds in employment in Liverpool were messenger boys and the figure was in excess of 40 per cent in Bootle, Blackpool, Southport, Manchester, Salford and Barrow; in contrast, only 5–8 per cent of boys of this age in the textile towns of Blackburn, Burnley, Oldham and Rochdale were messengers.[3] Without a strong manufacturing economy boys in large cities were dispersed into various service occupations.

The 'boy labour problem' can thus be seen to have been a city phenomenon, although the 'problem' existed to some degree in other towns. This is borne out by the fact that almost half the people who gave evidence to the Inter-Departmental Committee on the Employment of School Children in 1901–2 came from Manchester and Liverpool, and these cities, therefore, are particularly dominant in this chapter.

Concern about boy labour appeared to be stimulated by the sight of large numbers of boys seen in and around the streets learning nothing in respect of a skilled occupation, but being apparently physically and morally exploited by employers as cheap labour. It was, therefore, as much a criticism of employers as it was of the children involved. Increasing economic competition from overseas towards the end of the nineteenth century heightened insecurity in Britain and led to fears about moral decline, physical degeneration, unemployment and the country's role as the head of a large empire in the competitive world market. After thousands of recruits failed the physical examination to join the army in the Boer War, thoughts were even more concentrated on the well-being of future generations. The problem of 'boy labour' encapsulated all these concerns. Due to the large demand for boys, it was felt that boys were able to move from job to job, which led to a decline in discipline and training, while they received high wages, which was spent on unacceptable leisure pursuits. The casual, unskilled nature of much of the work also threatened to create future generations unable to compete in the international market, while undermining the jobs of skilled adults, thus creating unemployment. It was, according to Reginald Bray, little better than 'remunerative loafing' with no prospect of advancement beyond the 'dreary morass of unskilled labour'.[4] Youths in such occupations, especially street trading, were also thought to turn to crime when they did not have enough to sustain their needs. 'The tale of the boy's life is a series of unrelated incidents', concluded one writer; 'it needs to be unified by progressive organisation in the interests no less of national character than national economy.'[5] The belief that the boys and the country needed protection from 'blind alley' employment led to much literature on the subject as well as many official government enquiries, followed in some instances by legislation. This chapter will concentrate on those occupations which attracted the greatest criticism.

## *Street traders and newsboys*

Street trading was the most obvious aspect of this problem. All over the country lads found work on the streets. It is impossible to put precise figures on the numbers involved. They worked as hawkers selling anything from matches and ice-creams to flowers and hot peas. Some were knife

A Manchester newsboy, from R. Sherard's *Child Slaves of England* (1905). News vending attracted considerable criticism in the 1900s – the boy's arrogant stance and the cigarette suggest premature adulthood, while the newspapers he is selling expose him to unsavoury sensationalism. (London, Hurst & Blackett, facing page 91)

sharpeners, others organ grinders; yet others simply hung around waiting to run errands or carry luggage for people. In Liverpool, as no doubt in other towns, a regular job was knocking people up in the morning. Of all the street trades, however, selling newspapers was the most common amongst young boys. Many were concentrated in the major cities and public concern was focused here, but newspaper selling was undertaken in every town by young boys, many of whom were still at school and looking to earn a few extra pennies. One man from Preston recalls

The lads, if you had a penny, you would go to the *Lancashire Evening Post* and buy three for a penny. You would come out and sell them at a ha'penny a piece. You would get three

A newsboy plies his trade in Cheapside, Lancaster, *c.* 1905. (Lancaster City Council, Museums Service)

ha'pence then. Then you would go and get another penny-worth and you would end up with tuppence. In them days, everybody travelled by train, there weren't buses, so at Preston station, people that were coming in from Leyland and out-lying districts, all come off here and they all wanted the *Post*. If you could get six papers, you would sell them and you would have threepence. If you wanted to keep it up, you would keep on all night when you knew trains were coming in. I never did it a lot, but my mates did.[6]

The situation was similar in Barrow where one man recalled that his poorer pals got a dozen *Barrow Herald*s and sold them on the street to

Black pea seller, Accrington, c. 1900. Urban street traders supplied a wide range of goods and service. Children's involvement was frequently condemned, but those employed by their families, such as this young lad, were not considered to be exposed to the same moral dangers as those working independently. (Lancashire County Library, Accrington Local Studies Collection)

anybody by shouting. He once got a dozen papers, but his father heard him shouting and disapproved and he had to take them back. 'He (his father) was a bit higher than most people as a shopkeeper. Oh no, it was an unheard of thing.'[7] This account also points to the fact that newspaper selling was seen as very low status.

Street traders were not only regarded as unsightly; they were considered to fall prey to the temptations of life on the street, becoming associated with petty crime and begging. Those in authority also disliked the independence such boys seemed to have, and felt that they had no control over a lot of them. The Chief Constable of Manchester, in a paper to a Conference of Chief Constables in 1907, stated that 'street trading . . . is productive of a greater amount of evil, morally and physically than any other occupation followed by children. The boys develop into lazy, shiftless

and worthless men.'[8] Other commentators, however, were more concerned about the physical well-being of the boys on the streets who worked
long hours, often in bad weather and late into the night. Some not only
worked on the streets but lived in the open or spent their spare time just
hanging around on the corners.

The Employment of Children Act of 1903 attempted to regulate street
trading by prohibiting all those under eleven years from any selling, and
those under fourteen years from trading before 6 a.m. and after 9 p.m. In
Manchester and Liverpool, however, where the problem of street trading
was considered particularly severe, bye-laws had already been passed to
try and regulate it. The Manchester Corporation Act of 1901 had made it
illegal for children to trade on the streets without a licence and only those
over twelve years old were granted a licence. Even licensed children were
not allowed to trade after eight o'clock at night between 1 October and 31
March, or after nine o'clock at night between 1 April and 30 September.
Similar bye-laws had been included in the Liverpool Corporation Act of
1898 which made it illegal for boys under fourteen years and girls under sixteen years to trade on the streets without a licence, or to enter public houses.

However, these bye-laws were only partially effective. Parents paid little
attention to them and many children traded without licences or misrep-
resented their age to make sure they obtained a licence. Even with licences,
boys did not adhere to the stipulated hours and a lot still went into public
houses regardless. Children under the age of twelve years were often
reported as being on the streets selling late at night. Mr Patterson, a flour
and potato merchant with business in Liverpool, spoke particularly on this
subject when giving evidence to the enquiry into the Employment of
School Children in 1902. He stated that traders who were licensed to trade
by Liverpool Corporation had belts to wear, which they wore round their
necks, arms or waists. 'It is sometimes the only respectable piece of clothing
they have got, and it is practically a cloak for them.' He continued that
street trading 'does not injure me from a trade point of view, but from a
sentimental point of view I think it is a disgrace to the city of Liverpool to
see so many dirty, half-naked children run about the streets at all hours of
the day'.[9]

The problem persisted because children of the poor were often driven
on to the streets to help the family economy in these cities where regular

work for adults was difficult to obtain. Mr A. F. Browne, Manager and Trustee of the Liverpool News Boys' Home, pointed out that 'We find in our experience that children who sell papers are a great help to widowed mothers, or to mothers who have been left by drunken fathers'.[10] Writing of the turn of the century Manchester, Sherard observed that 'all the regulations in the world will not prevent them from disregarding the law when starvation and ill-treatment at home are the certain punishment which awaits them if they do not bring back a minimum of profit which too often represents a maximum of effort'.[11] Even magistrates in Liverpool often dealt leniently with those who broke the terms of the Corporation Act because they felt many boys had difficult conditions to contend with at home.

## Shop and errand boys

The late nineteenth century saw a massive expansion of the retail trade and increasing competition for custom, much of it based on offering personal service and deliveries. Cities like Liverpool and Manchester accommodated new large department stores catering for the middle class, while the Co-operative societies, which had originated in textile Lancashire and were very strong there, increasingly diversified their sales of products and services, and expanded their stores in all the manufacturing towns from the 1880s. Multiples, or 'chain stores', began to appear in high streets in the following decade. A variety of private shops existed, from small corner shops to established town-centre traders; a general shop was found on most street corners in the urban areas. Although large-scale retailers were significant in certain trades, these private shopkeepers still dominated retailing and accounted for over 80 per cent of total sales as late as 1910.[12]

Employment opportunities for boys in retailing were plenty and diverse. Many of them began by working before and after school. Bray estimated that in 1911 over 50 per cent of schoolchildren in part-time work in London were engaged in shop employment and 47 per cent of boys aged between fourteen and eighteen years worked in shops or transport.[13] Like the street trader, much work was out of doors. Boys were used to mind pavement displays or act as door-boys for high-class stores. Mr A. J. Johnston, Vice-President of the Liverpool Grocers and Provision Dealers' Association, stated at the inquiry on the Employment of School Children that he employed a thirteen or fourteen year-old boy on a Friday evening and all day Saturday. 'He (the boy) stands at the door principally, watching the goods; he has no selling to do; all he has to do is to draw the attention of customers anxious to buy.' A blind at the front of the shop protected him from bad weather. Mr Johnston continued that there were a great many of these boys in Liverpool 'and they stand outside all day summer and winter'.[14] Most boys were used to fetch and carry, or to run errands, since shops increased

Errand boys in St Leonardsgate, Lancaster. (Lancaster City Council, Museums Service)

their services, in particular deliveries, in an attempt to compete with each other. These had to be regular, fast and cheap and consequently, 'Every wire has a boy on the end of it'.[15] 'They are so convenient', remarked Helen Bosanquet, 'so easy to send and so cheap, that everyone likes to have one handy.'[16] One man from Lancaster recalls his first job very clearly.

> About nine years of age I started as an errand boy at a grocer's shop in Penny Street . . . I used to go straight from home right down to the shop, scrub out at the morning, I used to walk from there into Market Street down to the New Inn where the brewery is and I used to get two buckets of boiling hot water which was a penny each . . . I didn't scrub every morning of course, there was different duties and just before nine o'clock I used to get off to school . . . I went home

Going to market in Burnley. Boys were the fetchers and carriers for the increasingly commercialised society which emeged in the late nineteenth century. They ran errands, carried messages, delivered goods and acted as general dogsbodies for shopkeepers and local businesses. (Lancashire County Library, Burnley Local Studies Collection)

for tea and then I went down at night and did different jobs. If there were any errands to go I went errands.[17]

In Preston a man recalls that his brother ran errands for a confectioner's shop, carrying a sheep's head from the slaughter-house to the shop where it would be used for meat and potato pies.[18] Boiling beef and sausages were

The staff of Hey's general grocer's shop, Edward Street, Colne, resplendent in their working aprons. The young lad would probably have been employed packing, carrying, and delivering goods to local customers. (Lancashire County Library, Colne Local Studies Collection)

part of the wages for another boy in Barrow who delivered meat from the market on a Saturday to homes in the town.[19]

Some shop-related work, especially the delivery of milk, bread and newspapers, was largely done by schoolchildren out of school. The headmaster of Barrow Island Junior School in 1898 listed twenty-eight boys in his school aged between nine and thirteen years who were full-time scholars working for wages before and after school. Almost half of them were delivering milk and they worked from six hours to fifty hours per week, earning from 9*d.* to 6*s.* 6*d.*[20] A few years later the headmaster complained to the town's Director of Education that one employer was preventing two boys from being punctual at school, causing them to arrive without having eaten breakfast.[21] The Liverpool grocer, Mr Johnston, when asked if young boys were absolutely necessary for carrying on his trade, answered that it would be a great inconvenience without them since more expensive labour would have to be employed in the form of older boys. He continued, 'I may tell you that boys up to twelve years old we can easily get; but regular errand boys are most difficult to get, in fact we can get far more men of forty than lads of fourteen'.[22] Arguments such as this convinced the official government enquiry in 1902 and it reported that 'moderate' work for schoolchildren could be beneficial rather than harmful.

There were two major concerns regarding shop and errand boy employment for those who entered the trade after leaving school, however; firstly, the physical aspect of working long hours and carrying heavy loads, and secondly, the poor promotion prospects or possibility of moving into skilled employment. Full-time shop hours could be very long, up to eighty-four per week, and this compared unfavourably with factories where about sixty hours were worked by this time.[23] Boys went into the shop early to set up and stayed late to clear up, and many worked the Saturday afternoon which for other workers was a half-day holiday. Mr Johnston stressed this point; 'The (Saturday) afternoon is a period for recreation, and our lads are enough taunted with being tied as it is. Other lads as they pass say, "Are you going to Everton this afternoon?"' The lad thought his earnings 'very dearly bought when he has to sacrifice a Saturday afternoon's football'.[24] A Shops Act limiting the hours of children and young people who worked 'in and around shops' to seventy-four per week was passed in 1886 but there was no further legislation until after the First World War; a proposal to restrict hours of work for all shop assistants to sixty was removed from the Shops Act of 1911. The boys were also thought to suffer excessive hardship through standing on their feet all day inside the shop, or being 'harnessed between the shafts of a ponderous and heavily laden handcart or carrying excessively heavy baskets'.[25] Mr Johnston said that he limited his boy to carrying between fourteen to twenty pound parcels in a basket on his arm for a distance of 200 to 300 yards or a quarter of a mile at the outside, but whether others followed his example is far from clear.[26] Boys carrying baskets, pushing or pulling carts, or mounted on specially built bicycles are seen on many of the photographs of street scenes around the turn of the century.

It was acknowledged that boys often only took up shop employment for the short period after leaving school before they were able to enter a trade, but this still caused concern because it did not lead on to a future career. Some private traders and the Co-operative movement tried to offer boys better conditions and the chance to learn the skills of the trade and climb up a hierarchical ladder. The boy who delivered meat from Barrow market started working full-time in the boot shop at the Co-op at Barrow for 5s. a week, a total change in both wages, work environment and prospects from his previous part-time job.[27] But, as the Reverend Mr Spencer J. Gibb, who made many enquiries in the Manchester area, pointed out, 'the great majority of boys who enter upon the work of errand boys are offered and expect no prospect; learn nothing which will be of use to them; and begin, in short, a process of aimless drift from one job to another, the market value of their labour decreasing with increasing years'.[28] Though some boys did continue in the retail trade, for the majority of boys it was 'blind alley' employment with no chance to acquire knowledge about the products they were selling or distributing.

## Van boys

A further occupation which involved boys working on the streets of large cities was that of van boys or 'nippers'. In the port city of Liverpool in 1899, transport absorbed 30.6 per cent of school-leavers whereas transport in a provincial cotton town like Oldham absorbed only 1 per cent.[29] Manchester, too, had a great number of boys engaged in van, lorry or cart deliveries. The boy would accompany the driver, guard the van from theft or look after the horse, and assist the driver in the delivery of parcels. Not all reformers viewed this job in a poor light. Charles Russell, a promoter of boys' clubs in Manchester, observed that the van boy had to be able to read well enough to make out the addresses on the parcels and to be able to write legibly to fill out consignment notes. The open air was good for the boy, and he learned to use his wits, that is, in noting other possible openings for employment.[30] A few lines from a poem in *Punch* in 1912, written at the time that the government was mounting a national enquiry, also contain some positive views of the van boy.

He's small for his years but as sharp as a needle,
Accustomed to traffic before he could crawl,
He's a militant shrimp, and, like most of his breed,'ll
Lay odds on a dog-fight or corner street brawl . . .
His brain is alert, his anatomy plastic,
He has to nip back to his place how he can,
By dodges and tricks that are slim and gymnastic,
When left in the lurch by the vanishing van . . .[31]

But concern was expressed about the moral behaviour of the van boys and the physical effect of the work, the excessive hours and the limited prospects of this form of employment. J. G. Cloete, quoted in the Parliamentary Report into Boy Labour, stated that 'Van boys . . . are recruited chiefly from among the poorest classes . . . the work itself seems to have a far from elevating influence'. The report continued, 'The life of the van boy is a rough and somewhat lazy one. They have long hours, spells of idleness and considerable opportunities of pilfering and drinking.'[32] Russell added that the fault of the van boy was having no desire to improve himself, caring only for amusement in the form of theatre, music hall and football; an increasingly common criticism of all youth at this time.[33]

Trade unions in Liverpool and Manchester also expressed anxiety about the long hours van boys worked. 'Boys are treated worse than any class in Liverpool; they may be seen going home at 12 o' clock at night and are on at 8 o' clock next morning; this is quite common', remarked Mr Ditchfield of the Mersey Quay and Railway Carters' Union. His observations were echoed by Mr Hilton of the United Carriers' Association of England for the Manchester area. 'Boys can be seen at the stable any morning soon after 7 and anyone acquainted with Manchester streets can see them going home at 11 and 12 o'clock at night. With the exception of those employed in the centre of the town, I would imagine the normal day's work to be fifteen to sixteen hours . . . Schoolchildren employed by one firm are taken on after school and worked until 10 p.m. and on Saturdays from 7.30 a.m. until late on Saturday evenings.'[34] The hours worked, apart from being excessive, produced 'certain evil effects such as defective physique, and a general recklessness of character'.[35]

Russell considered that the van boy was seldom able to continue in the job after the age of seventeen years, and that carters, or carmen, were not usually appointed under the age of twenty-one years.[36] There was, therefore, an interval between adult employment and their previous occupation which did not prepare the van boys for any new type of work. The government Report on Boy Labour in 1909 concluded that being a van boy 'is a very low grade of occupation and that very few boys who begin as van boys get into skilled trades – a far lower percentage in fact than errand boys'.[37] In 1913 the Report on the Hours and Conditions of the Employment of Van Boys also found that the majority, though they were not dismissed from the job, drifted away as they got older, since businesses were incapable of absorbing or paying for them as 'adult' workers. The boys, therefore, tended 'towards unemployment at the age of nineteen'.[38]

## Post Office and clerical jobs

Two relatively new occupations which appeared to promise job security for boys, and which were seen by many parents as respectable employment, were those of clerk and Post Office telegraph boy. At the end of the nineteenth century the clerical labour force in Lancashire grew quite dramatically, especially in the thriving commercial centres of Liverpool and Manchester. In these cities, institutions connected with the exchange and sale of goods, like banks, brokers and insurance companies, expanded rapidly and took on more clerks, virtually all of whom were males. Elsewhere in Lancashire, the clerical labour force also grew with the expansion of local government, the railways and trade and commerce.

A distinguishing characteristic of this new labour force was its youthfulness. Employers were able to employ school-leavers because at school they had learned the basic skills needed for clerking: reading, writing and counting. In the survey of 1893–4, 23 per cent of the Liverpool school-leavers whose occupation was given, began work as clerks; in Manchester it was 25 per cent. Many boys, especially those from respectable working-class homes, were encouraged to become clerks by their parents, who thought that office work offered stability, economic reward, the chance of promotion and greater social status. Parents of boys taken on by large companies sometimes thought that their sons were becoming commercial apprentices rather than just clerks, and the boys themselves looked down at those who worked in shops, factories, workshops or on the streets.

Although clerical work was less physically demanding and offered better hours and working conditions than factory or shop work, it did not live up to the expectations of many children and their parents. Clerks were often little more than messenger boys and cleaners, sometimes employed on a temporary basis, and they usually earned less than Lancashire mill operatives who called the young clerks 'pen pushers' to insult them. Promotion was difficult. Boys who worked for large, expanding concerns had a better chance of being promoted than those in offices which were so small that there were few ranks to climb. Many boys found that the basic skills of reading and writing which they had acquired at school did not give them the ability to handle complex accounts and as a result they soon gave up on the idea of becoming adult clerks. Other school-leavers found that there was little scope for intelligence or initiative once the job had been learned and boredom soon set in.

At the end of the nineteenth century established clerks attacked what they called the 'apprenticeship' system for attracting so many young men into clerking and thereby 'undercutting wages, holding up the mobility of established clerks and generally lowering the status of the profession'.[39] To some extent their criticisms were justified as young men were taking over the profession. As early as 1871 B. G. Orchard, in his study of Liverpool clerks, estimated that out of 8,335 clerks, 3,952 of them were apprentices and 3,043 were office lads. The Liverpool Clerks' Association throughout the 1890s was responsible for placing more and more young clerks as apprentices but 'before long the number of situations being found for youths was exceeding the number of permanent positions being found for older members, a sure sign that Liverpool employers were turning to young cheap labour to run their offices'.[40] Clerking, therefore, was also viewed as a 'blind alley' occupation, with boys only taught what was necessary to do their job, the employer feeling under no obligation to offer further training. Boys were cheap and abundant, especially in Manchester and Liverpool, and this meant that employers could often discard their young clerks at the end of their apprenticeship.

A further occupation which left boys with no secure employment at the age of sixteen years was the Post Office. Telegraph boys or boy messengers were given the impression of permanence because it was government work. Many parents saw the Post Office as having good prospects for their sons and apparently many of 'the best lads attending elementary school'[41] and 'often the pick of the family'[42] went into this employment. Revd Spencer Gibb, reporting on Manchester, observed that the impression of permanence was heightened by the apparent care which was shown in the selection of messengers; these had to be a certain height, produce testimonials to their character, furnish a copy of their birth certificate and be medically sound and vaccinated.[43] Only a very small number, however, were absorbed into the adult service and the exploitation of these boys by the government, and the fact that so many boys were running around the streets, was criticised by many reformers.

Most boys from thirteen to fifteen were also employed as outdoor messengers on the streets, with very few inside; they were younger and earned a shilling less than the indoor boys who earned 8*s.* a week. Casual boy messengers were employed for a few weeks in June and July, when the telegraph business was under greater pressure, and also at Christmas to replace messengers who were doing temporary postal work. Bray did not consider the conditions of work to be good, with boys often idle for long periods.[44] This view was confirmed by the mother of a boy who was dismissed from the Post Office in 1901 for pranks; she was reported to have said that it was because her son worked only four and three-quarter hours out of the nine in a day and claimed that he had left the Post Office because 'time had hung heavily'.[45] In addition to not providing job security within the Post Office, messenger work did not train the boys for employment in any future trade. In areas where there was a strong manufacturing economy, unemployed telegraph boys could find work when they left. In Blackburn, for example, Post Office boys found employment as weavers; in Barrow, they became naval ordnance workers; and in Bolton, the Postmaster was reported to have obtained jobs for ex-messengers in the railway company. In the commercial cities of Liverpool and Manchester, however, the large number of ex-messengers and postboys found it difficult to secure further employment. In Manchester a boy of seventeen years who had been employed as an indoor messenger and discharged at the age of sixteen years wrote, 'What knowledge I had gained at the Post Office was useless elsewhere, often being told that they could get lads direct from school with equally as much knowledge as I must have'. A boy from Liverpool stated that he had to take low wages after being discharged from the Post Office, earning 5*s*. to 8*s*. when he could have been earning £1 per week in a trade. Charles Russell, from the Heywood Street Lads' Club in Manchester, argued that there was no worse employer of boy labour in the country than H. M. Government, whose treatment of telegraph messengers was 'simply deplorable', and Professor Sadler stated that government departments were to blame for the parasitic character of some forms of industry, which were an injury to national life 'in the using up of the physical and moral capital of the rising generation'.[46]

As a result of such attacks on the government, measures were introduced to reduce the number of boy messengers, and to absorb more into the Post Office or other Departments of State or to increase the boys' chances of outside employment. By 1915 the measures appeared to have been successful and a parliamentary Standing Committee reported that 'it was possible to absorb every boy messenger who was both willing and fit to enter the permanent service of the State; 52.6 per cent of boys ceasing to be messengers entered the public service'.[47]

## Seasonal work

This review of boys' work in Lancashire would be incomplete without reference to the casual, seasonal employment which was increasingly found in the growing seaside resorts, and Blackpool in particular. As towns which concentrated almost entirely on providing services, there were always shop boys, van boys and delivery boys but, with the arrival of tourists during the summer season, other businesses also took on more staff. Many boys found work in workshops making ice-cream and sweets, trading on the streets or carrying bags for tourists arriving at railway stations; many were temporary migrants and it was usually these outsiders who became street traders for the summer season. Tourist attractions, like the fifty-one acre Raikes Hall pleasure garden established in 1871, with its novelties which included a roller-skating rink, bicycle track and miniature railway, also employed boys by the dozen.

Barefooted, but presumably literate, street urchins in Liverpool. Child welfare agencies were particularly active in the city where a lack of regular industrial employment was contrasted with the ease with which casual work on the streets could be obtained from an early age. (Liverpool Record Office)

A major concern in seaside resorts was the high level of truancy throughout the holiday season. Local children stayed away from school to work for the summer, usually with their parents' permission. School log books reveal that attendances dipped dramatically in the summer months and only began to improve again in September. 'Blackpool schoolteachers awaited the autumn with trepidation as . . . the boys drifted into casual employment for the season.' Not all the boys who went to work in the holiday played truant. In fact 'the pressures of the popular industry were responsible for Blackpool becoming one of the last strongholds of the "half-timer" in the early twentieth century'.[48] Blackpool had one of the lowest partial exemption requirements in 1904–5, a mere 280 attendances per year (ie. the equivalent of 140 days) or the attainment of Standard IV. This allowed them to be absent from school for four full months each year, from the beginning of June to the end of September.[49] Mr H. M. Richards, giving evidence to the Inter-Departmental Committee on Partial Exemption from School Attendance in 1909 reported that such children were employed in domestic and company houses, or, even worse, 'minding stalls on the promenade and in the streets, and in selling picture postcards'. It was, he concluded, 'deleterious in every way'.[50]

## Conclusion

By focusing on occupations which attracted critical comment, it might appear that most boys at the turn of the century were running around the streets, earning easy money and then, by the age of sixteen years, finding themselves without a job and with few prospects. This was the picture painted by many reformers, but it was only part of the picture. We must not forget that many boys still took up apprenticeships in the heavy industries, as at Barrow where shipbuilding dominated, and in St Helens in the chemical and glass industries. The textile industry also absorbed the majority of school-leavers in east Lancashire towns, although as we have seen, this also attracted criticism.

But since many apprenticeships only began at fifteen or sixteen it was necessary for boys on leaving school to take up whatever work was available to them in their locality since they needed to earn money for their families before then. As this chapter has shown, work was not difficult to find. Russell commented, 'Boys can generally find employment of one kind or another within a few days of leaving school. Moreover they are guided by accident and circumstances rather than by preference. What most of them want is, not to learn a trade or industry, but to earn wages.'[51] After leaving school, many boys must have continued in the occupation which they had commenced whilst still at school. Thus the Lancaster boy, quoted earlier, who worked for a grocer whilst still at school, eventually went to work at the shop full-time. Many of the other jobs which attracted criticism provided work for those too young to enter skilled work. The highest percentage of boys occupied as messengers in 1911 was in the thirteen to fifteen age group and the figure declined rapidly from sixteen years upwards as boys entered other occupations.

Though the concern regarding boys' occupations was genuine, therefore, especially as regards the physical exploitation, and some of the problems were eventually addressed by legislation, the problem was more one of coming to terms with the changing face of labour brought about by economic developments rather than the children or the jobs themselves. In some respects, the growth of service jobs, especially in cities like Liverpool, could be seen as a distinct benefit, since it was a city which, as we have seen, had offered little in the way of employment to children in the mid-nineteenth century. In Lancashire, as elsewhere, it was not the boys who changed their demands for work before and after leaving school; economic change determined the jobs available and social change created anxieties which determined how those jobs were perceived.

## References

1.  C. H. Lee. 'The Service Sector, Regional Specialisation, and Economic Growth in the Victorian Economy', *Journal of Historical Geography* 10, ii (1984), p. 139.
2.  *Report on the Employment of Children on Leaving School*, PP, 1899, lxxv, pp. 484–581. The survey was extensive but was not a complete record of all schoolchildren.
3.  *Census of Great Britain, 1911*, Lancashire, Table 23: Occupations of Males and Females in County Boroughs.
4.  R. A. Bray, 'The Boy and the Family', in E. J. Urwick (ed.), *Studies of Boy Life in our Cities* (Dent, 1904), pp. 88–9.
5.  S. J. Gibb, 'Boy Labour: Some Studies in Detail', in J. H. Whitehouse (ed.), *Problems of Boy Life* (P. S. King, 1912), p. 78.
6.  Oral History Collection, CNWRS, Lancaster University, respondent G.1.P, p. 28.
7.  Oral History Collection, CNWRS, respondent H.2.B, pp. 74–5.
8.  *Report on the Inquiry into Boy Labour*, PP, 1909, xliv, p. 948.
9.  *Inter-departmental Committee on the Employment of School Children*, PP, 1902, xxv, pp. 451–2.
10. ibid., p. 460.
11. R. H. Sherard, *Child Slaves in Britain* (London, Hurst and Blackett, 1905), p. 211.
12. M. J. Winstanley, *The Shopkeeper's World 1830–1914* (Manchester University Press, 1983), p. 217.
13. R. A. Bray, *Boy Labour and Apprenticeship* (Constable, 1912), pp. 122–3.
14. *Employment of School Children*, PP, 1902, xxv, pp. 440–1.
15. Canon Scott Holland quoted in Bray, *Boy Labour*, p. 124.
16. H. Bosanquet, *The Standard of Life* (Macmillan & Co., 1898), p. 178.
17. Oral History Collection, CNWRS, respondent H.3.L, p. 1.
18. ibid., respondent C.1.P, p. 9.
19. ibid., respondent M.1.B, p. 4.

20. Barrow Island Junior (Boys) School log book, 20 June 1898, LRO, BDS/15.
21. ibid., 27 May 1908.
22. *Employment of School Children*, PP, 1902, xxv, p. 441.
23. *Select Committee on Shop Hours Regulation Bill*, PP, 1886, xii, p. 18.
24. *Employment of School Children*, PP, 1902, xxv, p. 441.
25. *Inquiry into Boy Labour*, PP, 1909, xliv, p. 946.
26. *Employment of School Children*, PP, 1902, xxv, p. 440.
27. Oral History Collection, CNWRS, respondent M.1.B, p. 4.
28. *Inquiry into Boy Labour*, PP, 1909, xliv, p. 944.
29. *Inquiry into Boy Labour*, PP, 1909, xliv, p. 928.
30. C. E. B. Russell, *Manchester Boys* (Manchester University Press, 1905), pp. 9–10.
31. *Punch*, 16 October 1912, p. 306.
32. *Inquiry into Boy Labour*, PP, 1909, xliv, p. 947.
33. Russell, *Manchester Boys*, pp. 10–11.
34. *Departmental Committee on the Hours and Conditions of the Employment of Van Boys and Warehouse Boys*, PP, 1913, xxxiii, p. 468.
35. ibid., p. 466.
36. Russell, *Manchester Boys*, p. 10.
37. *Inquiry into Boy Labour*, PP, 1909, xliv, p. 947.
38. *Hours and Conditions of Van Boys and Warehouse Boys*, PP, 1913, xxxiii, pp. 466–8.
39. G. Anderson, *Victorian Clerks* (Manchester University Press, 1976), p. 52.
40. ibid., p. 5.
41. *Inquiry into Boy Labour*, PP, 1909, xliv, p. 1036.
42. Bray, *Boy Labour*, p. 131.
43. *Inquiry into Boy Labour*, PP, 1909, xliv, p. 1025.
44. Bray, *Boy Labour*, p. 126.
45. *Inquiry into Boy Labour*, PP, 1909, xliv, p. 1016.
46. All quotations from evidence to *Inquiry into Boy Labour*, PP, 1909, xliv, pp. 1025–36.
47. *Standing Committee on Boy Labour in the Post Office*, Fifth Report, PP, 1914–16, xxxii, p. 987.
48. J. K. Walton, *The Blackpool Landlady* (Manchester University Press, 1978), p. 133.
49. *Annual Report of the Board of Education 1904–5*, PP, 1906, xxviii, p. 77.
50. *Inter-Departmental Committee on Partial Exemption from School Attendance*, PP, 1909, xvii, pp. 951–4.
51. *Inquiry into Boy Labour*, PP, 1909, xliv, p. 933.

Chapter 6

# Work fit for girls

*Janice Adams and Stella Clarkson*

A S WE have seen (chapter 1), girls had fewer opportunities to obtain paid work and the range of jobs which they did was narrower than boys' throughout the century. Victorian concern with respectability and morality led to legislation which prevented them from taking up certain kinds of employment and to a definite hierarchy of socially acceptable types of job, ranging from the acceptable to the stigmatised. Even where they worked in the same industries as boys they were often paid a much lower wage or failed to gain promotion.

Lancashire, however, had a higher proportion of girls working than other parts of the country. In 1851, for example, 33.7 per cent of girls aged 10–14 were in gainful employment in Lancashire, compared with a national figure of 19.9 per cent.[1] Some of these girls were to be found in a wide range of industrial jobs making ropes in Lancaster and Liverpool, paper in Darwen, pins in Warrington, boxes in Manchester, matches and tobacco products in Liverpool, glass in St Helens and sorting coal, as 'pit-brow lasses', in the Wigan area. The vast majority, however, over 70 per cent in 1851, were employed in textiles, especially weaving, and were concentrated in the cotton districts in the county. Elsewhere in Lancashire, therefore, the proportion of girls recorded as being in paid work was much lower. The 1911 census, which was the first to provide detailed figures for different towns, also clearly shows this. (see chapter 1, Table 1.4)

In towns with low figures for girls' employment, concern was sometimes expressed about the moral consequences of the sort of work which poor girls were obliged to take. Clara Collet, for example, reporting to the Royal

Pit brow lasses. Women and children were excluded from underground work in 1842, but continued to be employed sorting coal above ground, especially in south-west Lancashire where they accounted for over twenty per cent of surface workers in the 1880s. Young girls were rarely employed, the vast majority of workers being single women aged between sixteen and thirty. (John Hannavy Picture Collection)

Commission on Labour in 1893, commented on 'the large class of women and girls in Liverpool who pick up a living by odd jobs which fall to their lot' and 'the dislike of regular work, which prevents even children who have just left school from seeking regular employment, and incites them to begin their industrial life as hawkers or cleaners for neighbours'.[2] The lack of other forms of employment in Liverpool encouraged more girls to take up street trading, selling a variety of goods, including flowers, matches, firewood and newspapers. It was often hard and heavy work especially for those who sold firewood, who were known as 'chip-girls'. They usually worked in teams, with one carrying the basket, containing about eighty bundles of wood, which the other girl would help to sell. Miss F. Melly, a member of the Liverpool School Board, giving evidence to the enquiry into the Employment of School Children in 1902, stated that two hours' work in the evening could earn the girls one shilling, and on Saturdays, if they worked from two till nine, they might earn two shillings between them. Children as young as six were identified as being involved in such work. This street trading by girls led to fears about their exposure to moral danger and claims that 'many of the girls were practically prostitutes using their ostensible trade as a cloak – and a very effective one – for prostitution and blackmail'.[3] Following the 1903 Employment of School Children Act several local authorities passed bye-laws restricting street trading by young persons; by 1907, girls under sixteen were prohibited from any street trading in Blackburn, Bolton, Burnley and Nelson, although these towns permitted trade when the girls were accompanied by a parent or guardian. In Preston, however, even this was prohibited. Blackpool, Bootle, St. Helens, Warrington and Widnes operated a partial ban prohibiting girls from trading in certain areas although Liverpool, which had first introduced regulation of street trading, did not act to exclude girls until 1911.[4]

But such occupations were limited to a minority of girls and there was not the same concern expressed about the work which they did as there was about boys' unskilled, casual labour. Outside the textile towns, girls who worked were largely restricted to a few occupations which were recognised as 'women's work', especially domestic service and dress-making. The majority undertook unpaid, 'invisible' work within their family homes, and such work was unrecorded by census enumerators and most official investigators. Neither the type of paid work which girls did, nor this hidden workforce, excited much comment for it was all considered either as part of a girl's duty towards her family, or as providing training needed to fulfil her 'proper' role in life as a wife and mother. The fact that they were not receiving industrial training for later employment, therefore, was less important; indeed, the waged work in textile factories was sometimes seen as detrimental since it prevented them from learning household skills.

Since textiles and agriculture have been dealt with elsewhere in the book, this chapter will concentrate on some of the other occupations which were available to girls, including not only traditional, female domestic work but also some of the newer opportunities in professions like teaching that became available towards the end of the century.

## *Home duties*

There was no record made of the many girls who worked at home because they were 'unwaged' and did not count as part of the official figures on employment. This did not mean that they did not undertake heavy manual work, or take on responsibility for bringing up the rest of the family, only that they were not officially recorded as workers. Indeed, the inquiry into schoolchildren's work in 1902 concluded that

> The severest work, the longest hours, and the hardest conditions are often found in the case of children who are employed without wages in doing housework in the homes of their parents. Many witnesses spoke strongly of the injury done in this way to girls, but all admitted that they could suggest no remedy.[5]

It was not unusual for girls to miss schooling through the need to help out at home. A teacher at Ulverston Girls' School, for example, wrote in May 1864 'The school very thin, the third of the girls absent, on account of the cleaning for Whitsuntide. A great many of their mothers go out to work', and again in June 1865; 'Attendance moderate, many of the girls kept home to nurse, while their mothers went out to work'.[6] Girls as young as seven or eight were often used as unpaid domestic servants. Angus Reach, a journalist reporting on the textile districts for the London newspaper the *Morning Chronicle*, encountered two young girls in Oldham in 1849, 'the eldest not above eight years of age, each carrying a baby some three or four months old'. On enquiring he was told that they were paid to look after the children whilst the mothers were at work; 'they pay us 1*s.* 6*d.* a week for each baby'. The little girls collected the babies in the morning, took them to the mill at lunch-time so that the mothers could breast-feed them, then returned them to their homes at night. They also said that sometimes 'the babies have little sisters, as old as us, and then they are nursed at home'.[7]

Oral history is one of the few sources of information on the domestic work which very young girls did although it only covers the late nineteenth century and early twentieth century. One lady from Barrow, born in 1895, said that she 'minded' her seven younger siblings, 'Oh minding babies, I didn't only do it for my mother, but I did it for my auntie as well'.[8] Another respondent, also born in Barrow in 1888, whose mother had sixteen children, said, 'We didn't go to school all the time. It was optional. She always kept one at home to mind the babies. She had to.'9 Children also often helped out in the family business, officially unrecorded and unrewarded. In 1905 Stella Davies' family ran a branch telephone exchange from their house at Heaton Moor near Manchester, and one of the conditions of being granted permission to operate it was that it would be attended twenty-four hours a day. As Mrs Davies was not very strong the three children, including Stella, aged twelve, and her sister aged ten, took it in turn to man the exchange once the day staff had left at eight p.m.[10]

Children may also have stayed off school to help out a working neighbour and those who did such forms of domestic work were not always paid. The inquiry of 1902 also had doubts about this sort of part-time work since it was often 'in very poor houses, and they are in many cases kept at it for undue hours and subjected to severe strain'.[11] Sherard, writing in the 1900s, commented that 'hard nanny' girls, employed in doorstep cleaning, 'the lowest work that any girl can be employed in — even worse than selling chips [ie firewood]' were often 'paid with crusts of bread'.[12] Other children worked for goods such as milk, eggs, meat, flour, coal, anything that was difficult for a very poor family to find the money for and that the child could take home to help the family economy. Another source of hidden work in the home was the use of poorer relatives as domestic servants.[13] These may have been given board and lodgings in exchange for help in the house, but they may not have been paid as such.

## *Domestic service*

The full-time equivalent of this form of work was domestic service and, outside the textile towns, this was the most important source of employment for girls on leaving school.[14] Jobs were easily found privately, through personal recommendation, through advertisements or an employment registry, or even in some districts at hiring fairs, like the one at Ulverston. By the end of the century, domestic servants were the largest group of female workers unprotected by a factory act or subject to a Board of Trade investigation. Private domestic service, however, became less important

Playing mother and collecting water (*above and opposite*)
During the 1920s the Lancaster photographer Sam Thompson captured the
flavour of life in the town's cramped, insanitary yards. These two illustrations
show young girls at play and involved in the regular chore of collecting water
for household use. (Lancaster City Council, Museums Service)

for 10–14 year-olds in Lancashire as the century progressed. Over 18.18
per cent of employed 10–14 year-old girls were domestic servants in 1851,
but by 1901 the figure had dropped to just 8.76 per cent and was to fall
still further to 5.73 per cent ten years later.

Domestic service was resorted to by many girls as a means of getting
pocket money while at school but there was no guarantee that they would
take this up full-time, perhaps because their experiences of the potential
hardships awaiting most young girls entering domestic service made them
prefer 'other forms of occupation'.[15] Margaret Penn, for example, had
worked each morning before school and all day Saturday at the local
vicarage for the small payment of ninepence per week when she was
twelve. She had all the hard, dirty jobs to do but she was delighted to be
earning her own money, although her mother was scandalised at the

Bristle picking, 1906. Women dominated the numerous, low paid, home-based sweated industries and they often relied on their children to assist them with menial or repetitive tasks. In 1906 *The Daily News* organised an exhibition, accompanied by an illustrated booklet and a series of lectures and practical demonstrations, to draw attention to the plight of such workers. Bristles were used for a wide range of household and industrial brushes; pickers and sorters were estimated to earn about twelve shillings a week if they worked twelve-hour days. (*Daily News* Sweated Industries Exhibition, Queen's Hall; catalogue. Photograph courtesy of City of Salford, Working Class Movement Library)

meagre payment she received. When it came time to leave school at the age of thirteen, however, Margaret refused to stay on at the vicarage full-time. 'To work at the vicarage, of her own free will, for extra spending-money was a different matter from working there, of necessity, as a servant'.[16]

Some considered service to be particularly suitable for a young working-class girl as it would give her a sound training for her later life as a wife and a mother. In 1857 J. D. Milne, author of *The Industrial and Social*

Girls learning how to make children's bodices at a Liverpool school, *c.* 1914. From the late nineteeenth century increasing attention was paid to training girls in those habits and skills which were deemed necessary for successful household management. These included cooking, laundry work, needlework and, as in this case, elementary dress-making. (Liverpool Record Office)

*Position of Women,* summarised idealised, middle-class attitudes to domestic service when he wrote, 'The situation of a domestic servant . . . is attended with considerable comfort. With abundant work it combines a wonderful degree of liberty, discipline, health, physical comfort, good example, regularity, room for advancement, encouragement to acquire saving habits.'[17] One male oral history respondent from Barrow echoed these views; 'It was a good thing to have the experience of being in service because a man would more readily marry a girl who was domesticated in that way than a girl who knew nothing about it'.[18]

These attitudes contrasted with those expressed about girls who worked in mills, many of whom were thought by the middle classes to lack the training, the time and energy to look after the homes properly. In textile areas most girls and their families chose to work in the factories. 'Domestic service might be cleaner and less dangerous than mill work, but few Lancashire girls opted for its low wages, long hours and restrictions on their freedom when they could earn so much more in a nearby mill.'[19] Consequently, employers preferred, or were obliged, to recruit servants from outside the area although this may not have been as true of places like Preston, where Willoughby's survey of household servants from the 1851 census found that the majority were local girls, perhaps a reflection that Preston was also a middle-class professional and market town before it was a mill town.[20]

Domestic service was thought to be such suitable employment for working-class girls that some special schools were established to train prospective servants. In Lancaster, a Charity School on High Street was founded in 1772 where girls between the ages of nine and eleven years were educated principally to become domestic servants. By the 1840s the school was still little more than a training school for household servants; at the age of twelve they were sent out as servants to subscribers of the charity, the girl herself receiving 1d. per week while the subscriber paid 1s. to the school for her services. Although the school gradually taught a wider curriculum from the 1870s, it continued to educate girls with the expectation that they would go into service when they left, until it was taken over by the Lancaster School Board in 1896.[21] Another training school was at Walkden Moor, Manchester where Lady Francis Egerton, wife of the owner of Worsley collieries, started Walkden Moor Servants' School in 1842 to train miners' daughters who were no longer able to work as pit girls.[22] The rules for this school mirrored the strictures under which a girl would eventually have to work. Every second of the day, from the rising-bell at 5.30 a.m. to lights out was accounted for, the menu for every day of the week was laid down in the rules, and clothing was specified down to the last pair of stays.[23] The curriculum in all the state and church schools which were established during the century also emphasised the need to train girls in domestic management, to fit them for being servants, wives and mothers. The Board of Education booklet, *Suggestions for Teachers* (1905), argued that schools should provide courses 'to fit girls to undertake when they leave the school the various household duties which fall more or less to all women'.[24]

Whether girls went into domestic service or stayed at home depended on a number of factors. Parents were often relieved when a daughter went away into service if the family could not afford to feed and clothe her. Since she was paid a wage, some money might find its way back to the family home. Some also hoped that the girls could better themselves by association, for they could experience a different way of life. Some of the girls, too, felt they were potentially moving up the social scale, if only by association. Margaret Penn's recollections of her experiences in Hollins Green, near Manchester, in 1910 suggest this. 'On the whole her work at the Vicarage had improved her. She had learnt easily to speak a fair imitation of Miss Brown's genteel speech. She now knew how to set a table neatly and accurately . . . and could now eat and drink and handle a knife and fork as expertly as that lady herself.'[25]

Some historians consider 'the best index of middle-class status in Victorian England was the keeping of a servant, since any middle-class man "'shrank'" . . . from reducing his wife to the level of a "drudge"'.[26] Others have qualified this. Edward Higgs, in his study of mid-nineteenth century Rochdale, argued that many were kept because they were needed to help in businesses which were run from the home; over a third of the households employing servants were farmers or retailers.[27] Willoughby in her thesis on Preston also showed that servants were employed to perform specific duties, rather than simply as status symbols and that 'domestic drudgery, spartan accommodation and physical abuse endured by many is scarcely synonymous with the concept of the servant as a status symbol'.[28]

In reality not all domestic servants were treated in the idealised manner suggested by Mr Milne. Domestic work varied a great deal depending on who and where the employer was, but since nineteenth-century Lancashire had a relatively small number of upper-class households, many young girls, 'slaveys' and 'tweenies', were probably the skivvies in lower middle-class homes. Servants were often badly housed, badly fed and badly clothed, and the work was of the most arduous kind. Living-in meant that the girl was fed and clothed by her employers, although 'clothed' sometimes meant even more work. Lewis's department store in Liverpool, for example, made up Christmas gift parcels for employers to give to servants which comprised material suitable for uniforms and 'some handkerchiefs thrown in to promote good-will at the festive season'.[29]

Even living and working in a 'big house' was very hard work. 'Like the working-class housewife, the servant girl's life was one long battle against dirt and disorder. The draughty Victorian mansions . . . required a continual onslaught of cleaning and polishing. Hours were long and pay was extremely low. Not for nothing were maids-of-all-work known as "slaveys".'[30] Girls were often taken advantage of physically, financially and sometimes morally, since by living in the home of a stranger young girls were put, or put themselves, in a situation that was open to abuse. It is, perhaps, not surprising, therefore, that girls increasingly sought other forms of work.

## *Hotel and guest houses*

By the late nineteenth century, work in hotels, inns, lodging- and boarding-houses was a rising source of girls' employment; unlike private domestic service, this type of work increased at a faster rate than population growth.[31] By the eve of the First World War, Liverpool alone had eighty-one hotels offering a range of employment for females as servants, cooks, kitchen and bar maids, and waitresses.[32] The growth in the hotel trade was also in part a result of the growth of the seaside and leisure industry. The work was similar to traditional service in many respects, and girls could be little better than maids-of-all-work as Lavinia Swainbank discovered, in the early twentieth century, when she was employed in a Windermere hotel at the age of sixteen. She worked at a variety of tasks from 6.30 a.m. to 10.00 p.m., including carrying luggage, cleaning shoes, emptying slops and helping in the kitchen. The 'live-in' conditions were poor, and she was expected to share a bed with the kitchen maid.[33]

Girls could find such employment in a number of ways including hiring fairs. Although these were used predominantly by those looking for farm-workers, they were not confined to this purpose, and employers from Cumberland, Lancashire and Westmorland wanting girls for hotel work made use of the one at Ulverston in particular; employers came from all parts of these counties. Hirings occurred twice a year in May and November with girls largely engaged for hotel work in May ready for the start of the season. In the 1890s they would have been contracted for half a year's employment for between three and six pounds, plus board and lodging. Agencies were another source of work for girls from the industrial towns and rural districts who sought seasonal employment in the rapidly developing seaside resorts. Advertisements were then placed in local papers, advising prospective employers that girls were available from as far afield as Lincoln and York; Manchester acted as the regional centre for such agencies.

Whilst the Lancashire seaside towns imported a number of girls to work in the holiday trade the majority were local, for many of the smaller boarding-houses could not afford to employ staff, and members of the family were often expected to fulfil this role. As a result approximately 40 per cent of Blackpool's female school-leavers in 1914 went into 'home duties'.[34] Many girls began such work prior to leaving school, however, or were in some way engaged in a range of other tourist industries. Blackpool and Morecambe were amongst the last towns to abolish the partial-exemption system. Morecambe had a very low qualifying standard which allowed twelve year-olds to be absent from the beginning of June to the end of September every year if they had reached Standard V or made only 250 attendances (i.e. 125 days) during the winter months.[35] The number of girls attending school consequently declined as the holiday season approached and they did not return until September when it was necessary for the schools formally to insist upon their return. The log book of St John's school for 23 September 1868 records: 'Today lists prepared of boys and girls who had been absent all the summer and pupil-teacher sent to call upon the parent requesting their attendance'.[36] In Morecambe attendance at the Poulton Road Girls' School had fallen so dramatically during June 1891 that instead of the normal 205 children there were a mere 122. The school log book records, 'Many of the elder girls have obtained permission from the board to be absent until the end of September'.[37] An entry for October 1896 demonstrated the problem that occurred when education was so disrupted. 'Many of the girls in Standard Six who have been absent all summer have now returned for the winter months. Four months of the school year has now passed but we must begin all their work again.'[38] It would appear that it was not always considered of primary importance to obtain official leaving or exemption certificates since many of the girls in both towns continued to work without them. The hours of work could be long and were initially unregulated and some expressed fears that girls in Morecambe were working in public places, such as the piers, music-halls and bazaars, which was considered not only 'wretched training for the future' but exposing them to moral dangers.[39]


## *Shop work*

Shop work was viewed as a male occupation until the latter part of the century but, as the trade expanded from the 1860s, a number of older girls joined the workforce after leaving school. As with domestic service, however, the proportion of girls in towns like Liverpool who entered shop work was significantly higher than in textile Lancashire towns. This reflected the growth of shops catering for a middle-class consumer society in the bigger cities and resorts, as well as the shortage of other 'respectable' jobs in such towns. But the sale of mass-produced, pre-packaged goods, which stimulated the development of these stores also encouraged the growth of small shops. Girls provided these shopkeepers with a cheap labour force. Their hours were often very long and were not effectively controlled by legislation; the Shop Hours Regulation Act of 1886 simply stated that 'A young person under 18 years of age must not be employed in or about a shop for more than seventy-four hours, including meal times, in any one week'. However, members of the shopkeeper's family were not even covered by this legislation, and could be employed at his discretion.

In the large cities, department stores like Lewis's offered a specific kind of employment. Girls could begin work in such stores from the age of fourteen. A number of stores and drapers' shops still relied on staff 'living-in' into the twentieth century, providing both food and lodgings for their staff, and thus reduced rates of pay. Liverpool Education Committee in their *Handbook of Employments*, for school-leavers, advised girls against working for firms who operated such a system. They warned that 'The food and sleeping accommodation are sometimes very poor, and, the assistants being on the premises, the hours of work may be unduly long. Girls would be well advised to seek employment where they may go home at night'.[40] Even assistants who did not live in could also work very long hours, from 8.30 a.m. to 8.00 p.m. and even 10.00 p.m. on Saturdays.

Stella Davies recalls that her seventeen year-old sister, who in 1900 worked at Lewis's Manchester store which had opened in 1880,

> would arrive home at nearly midnight, having walked the mile from the tram to our house and after having been on her feet all the long day (shop assistants were not allowed to sit down in view of customers) exhausted to breaking point. She would weep with weariness and although hungry be too tired to eat her supper. She would perk up a bit on Sunday but obviously dreaded the return to work on Monday.[41]

Some drapers' shops were reported as operating a system of fines from one penny upwards which could be levied for misdemeanours ranging from lateness, to failing to secure a sale, while conditions in the small shops were hardly better, with long hours and limited prospects. Despite all this, some girls preferred it to alternative employment where the pay could be higher and the hours shorter. This was because of shop work's reputation for being respectable and genteel, as acknowledged by one of the Barrow women, questioned by Elizabeth Roberts in her oral history study, who commented that 'You thought you were somebody'.[42] Alice Foley, upon leaving school at fourteen in 1904, chose to work in a fancy goods shop in Bolton for similar reasons. She earned 4s. a week, which appears to have been above the average for such work, no doubt a reflection of the higher wages paid to girls who worked in the town's textile industry.

## Tailoring and dress-making

Dress-making and, to a lesser extent, tailoring were often chosen by the girls against the wishes of poor parents, since there was normally an unpaid apprenticeship of two or three years and then a low wage for several more. Margaret Penn recalls in her autobiographical novel that she had to fight to be allowed to enter dress-making instead of domestic service. Her mother thought that 'book-reading had put all sorts of uppish ideas into her head'. However, her tears eventually won and she was apprenticed to the village dress-maker for two years and later transferred to a store in Manchester where she was told, 'We are Court Dressmakers here . . .

and only do the very best work. And you would have to be apprenticed to us for three years before beginning to earn anything.'[43] Mrs Hewitson was apprenticed to a Barrow dress-maker in 1898, at the age of thirteen. She recalled that she served her apprenticeship for over two years before she received her first wage of ten shillings and that she never had holidays except Bank Holidays.[44] In 1904 the Co-operative Society in Kirkby in Furness, a highly regarded employer, was engaging girls to work as apprentices in the millinery and drapery departments and paying them as first-year apprentices (a term they interchanged with assistants) the sum of 2*s.* per week. This training period lasted for two years, but upon completion not all girls were guaranteed further employment and some were dismissed.[45]

Because of the increasing demand for fashionable clothes, however, there was always the possibility of a trained girl eventually setting up her own business. This, and the opportunity to work in a 'creative' sphere and to learn a useful skill, attracted some girls away from the higher paid mill-work or domestic service, and dress-making was an expanding occupation by the end of the century.

There were several levels of employment, each one progressively more difficult to enter but each one offering increasing respectability. Manchester and Liverpool were centres of the sweated needle trades, and girls were often overworked and underpaid; many tailoresses, especially those working irregularly at home or in the back-street sweated workshops were invisible to inspectors from the Board of Trade. Liverpool's *Handbook of Employments* (1916) suggested that girls who entered the tailoring trade could expect to earn three shillings a week, or even 'work three months without wages, then start at 2*s.* 6*d.* per week', but warned that 'there are some firms of low standing which dismiss girls at the end of three months as incompetent, and so secure a constant supply of free labour'.[46] The handbook listed 574 tailoring firms, employing 933 girls, and 417 dress-making firms, employing 1,259 girls, in Liverpool. Other sewing trades, prone to exploitation through outwork and sweat-shops, were millinery, tie-making, shirt-making and clothing. Nearly 1,600 young girls were employed in these in Liverpool although increasingly such occupations were moving out of the home and workshop and into the factory. Elsewhere in Lancashire self-employed local dress-makers might employ a girl in their own homes and gave a basic training; those who copied the Paris fashions trained girls thoroughly on their shop premises, as did original designers in their own workshop.

## Pupil-teachers

Teaching, however, was perhaps the most prestigious expanding occupation for girls in the late nineteenth century. Sandon's 1876 Education Act had empowered District Education Committees to introduce compulsory education at a local level and Mundella's Education Act in 1880 had made education compulsory for all 5–10 year-olds throughout the country. The school leaving age was then progressively raised until by 1918 all children were obliged to attend full-time until they were fourteen.

The introduction and expansion of compulsory education created a huge demand for elementary school teachers and assistants. An increasing number of young girls joined a government-initiated apprenticeship scheme which had begun in 1846. This apprenticeship, or pupil-teacher scheme, was available to both sexes, but by the 1870s it had become a predominantly female route to a career. A survey of the employment of school-leavers in 1893–4 recorded that eighteen per cent of Barrow girls who left school and for whom an occupation was recorded entered teaching.[47] Eighty-seven per cent of those under twenty who were recorded in the 1901 census as teachers in Lancashire were female.[48] Some began at the age of twelve as monitors before being apprenticed from thirteen (fourteen from 1877) as pupil-teachers, acting as classroom assistants while continuing their studies part-time. Those who successfully completed the apprenticeship had the opportunity from the age of eighteen to attend a training college such as the one at Edge Hill in Liverpool, to become trained, certificated teachers. Males were more likely to continue to this final stage, however, while girls tended to study part-time for a certificate or simply sought employment as a teacher. Since the expansion of elementary schooling meant this was relatively easy, the proportion of female teachers who were 'unqualified' rose substantially nationally from 13 per cent in 1875 to 41 per cent in 1914 (9 per cent and 12 per cent for men).[49] This meant that girls were more likely to leave the profession, or remained as assistant teachers with lower salaries, since they had less chance of promotion.

Nassau Senior, shortly after the introduction of the pupil-teacher scheme, observed that it was 'a system of the highest pressure'.[50] Little changed throughout the century, for a great deal was demanded of pupil-teachers, and concern was expressed in the Pupil-Teacher Report of 1898 that they were grossly overworked.[51] Although apprentices had to be certified fit by a doctor, school log books reveal that a number suffered continuing ill-health, in part a consequence of the pressure under which they worked. Lily Charlesworth, a monitor at the Wesleyan Day School in Blackpool, was one of those who became too ill to continue, to the great regret of the headmaster who considered her an excellent prospect.[52] The pressure on girls appears to have been greater than on boys because, not only could they be expected to teach full-time whilst preparing for pupil-teacher examinations but, unlike their male counterparts, they were often expected to fulfil domestic duties at home. In 1846 monitors received payment of £5 for the first year; by 1878 when Annie Parkinson was appointed at Poulton Road Girls' School in Morecambe, she received £7 10s., paid quarterly.[53] Annie became a pupil-teacher in 1879 and would have received a wage increase, which would have then risen annually throughout her apprenticeship.[54]

Pupil-teachers, despite regulations controlling their work, were often used as full-time teachers, though many were ill-equipped for the job. Theresa Billington, for example, whilst a pupil-teacher in Blackburn, was expected to control a class of forty girls only a year or two her junior.[55] Pupil-teachers could even be left in charge of the school as noted in school log books: 'Annie Parkinson away; taking charge of Bare School'.[56] Annie at this time was a third-year pupil-teacher and was probably little more than sixteen, and the only help she received was from a young monitor. The understaffing increased since school attendance outgrew staff capabilities as the leaving age was gradually raised. One hundred and thirty children attending the Wesleyan Day School, Blackpool in 1880 were taught by the headmaster, a second- and first-year pupil-teacher and a temporary monitor. It can be no surprise that the head regularly bemoaned the quality of the lessons given by the apprentices, calling them ill-prepared. The classes, however, were subject to inspection and criticism by Schools

Miss Gertrude Washington's class at St John's Great Marsden Church of England School, Nelson, *c.* 1915. Nursing's importance and prestige were increasing before 1914 but were greatly enhanced by the experiences of war. (Lancashire County Library, Nelson Local Studies Collection)

Inspectors, a nerve-wracking experience which further increased the pressure upon the young teachers. Margaret Penn records how, when she was at school, even a fully-trained, certificated teacher was reduced to tears by the tension caused by the inspector's testing of her class.[57]

To comply with the terms of their apprenticeship the pupil-teachers needed to continue their own education. They were given extra lessons in a number of subjects, ranging from Latin to sewing (for girls only) usually prior to school opening, although chemistry was taught to pupil-teachers in Chapel Street in Blackpool from 6.30 p.m. to 9.00 p.m. on Saturdays.[58] They were also required to do homework and the head of the school, who was responsible for their training, could subject them to fortnightly examinations. Formal examinations would be carried out twice yearly in October and March, the results of which would determine whether they could continue their employment.

The pupil-teacher system was phased out in 1907, in favour of a bursary system. Girls then had to attend secondary school until they were sixteen, and training became more centred on specialist colleges. While the pupil-teacher scheme had been seen as a means of raising the social and economic status of working-class girls, the increased length and cost of attending school and college made teaching less accessible while raising the appeal of the profession for middle-class girls.

## Conclusion

Concern with respectability and morality, and preconceptions about what a woman's role in life was, affected the work girls did on leaving school as much as any changes in the economy or job market. Legislation banning 'unsuitable' employment for girls, like underground work in mines in 1842, meant some areas were closed to them, while jobs such as street trading had minimum age limitations placed on them, although these were often ignored. Some girls were able to find socially acceptable employment other than domestic work, but as these jobs normally involved some form of training, and during the training period there was little or no wage paid, the majority of working-class girls could not seriously consider such a course since many families could not wait any longer for their daughter to bring in a wage, or afford to pay for further training. To work in a store it was necessary to be able to dress appropriately. To become a dress-maker's apprentice it was often essential to be able to work without pay for several years. To become a teacher it was necessary to be academically qualified, something that the poorer children, who had taken time out of school for work, were unlikely to be. All this meant that it was girls in the upper working-class and lower middle-class families whose finances were relatively sound who were largely able to take on such work.

Some girls were kept at home to assist in the house while low pay and long hours were the lot of working girls, whatever employment they chose to go into. Despite legislation controlling 'abuses', most girls worked in unregulated environments in shops, sweated workshops, hotels and private houses. The wages of these women and young girls were far lower than the wages of males throughout the period, even in skilled, relatively prestigious jobs such as teaching, and reflected the social expectation that girls would not stay in such jobs as their real place was at home and that they would not be expected, therefore, to be family breadwinners.

By the 1900s only a few girls under fourteen were in full-time work, but half-timers in cotton mills were not the only ones who engaged in part-time work. There were many who worked unofficially before and after school or helped in family businesses like guest houses in seaside resorts. Even more were kept away simply to look after younger children or assist with the housework, since it was considered less important for girls to obtain an academic education and their services were extremely valuable in the home. Others often made their own employment by helping out neighbours and doing odd jobs. Just as today, children worked to help the family economy or to give themselves some financial freedom, and, just as today, their need to earn money was often exploited.

## References

1. H. Cunningham, 'The Employment and Unemployment of Children in England, *c*.1680–1851', *Past and Present*, 126 (1990), p. 145.
2. *Royal Commission on Labour, Reports on the Employment of Women*, PP, 1893–4, xxxvii, Part I, Miss Clara Collet (Assistant Commissioner) on the Condition of Work in Liverpool and Manchester, pp. 545–6.
3. *Report of the Inter-Departmental Committee on the Employment of School Children*, PP, 1902, xxv, p. 711.
4. *Return of Authorities who have made Bye-Laws Forbidding Street Trading under the Employment of School Children Act, 1903*, PP, 1907, lxxii, p. 329.
5. *Report on the Employment of School Children*, PP, 1902, xxv, p. 274.
6. Ulverston Girls' School log book, 13 May 1864, 21 June 1865, LRO, SMVI/1
7. A. B. Reach (ed. C. Aspin), *Manchester and the Textile Districts in 1849* (Helmshore Local History Society, 1972), p. 81.
8. E. Roberts, *A Woman's Place: an Oral History of Working-Class Women 1890–1940* (Blackwell, 1984), p. 23.
9. ibid., p. 34
10. C. S. Davies, *North Country Bred: a Working-class Family Chronicle* (Routledge and Kegan Paul, 1963), p. 79.
11. *Report on the Employment of School Children*, PP, 1902, xxv, p. 274.
12. R. H. Sherard, *The Child Slaves of Britain* (Hurst, 1905), pp. 233, 244.
13. E. Higgs, 'Women, Occupations and Work in the Nineteenth-Century Censuses', *History Workshop*, 23 (1987), p. 71.
14. *Return on Elementary Schools (Children Working for Wages)*, PP, 1899, lxxv, p. 562ff.

15. C. V. Butler, *Domestic Service* (Bell & Sons, 1916), p. 130.
16. M. Penn, *Manchester Fourteen Miles* (Cambridge, 1947, repr. Firle, Sussex: Caliban Books, 1979), pp. 198–9, 203.
17. Quoted in J. M. Golby (ed.), *Culture and Society in Britain 1850–1890* (Oxford, 1986), p. 11.
18. Roberts, *A Woman's Place*, p. 54.
19. J. Liddington and J. Norris, *One Hand Tied Behind Us* (Virago, 1985), p. 101.
20. S. A. Willoughby, 'Domestic Service and the Middle Class in Mid-Nineteenth Century Preston' (unpublished M.A. dissertation, University of Lancaster, 1987), p. 34.
21. G. G. Gregg, *Schools and Education in Lancaster* (Lancaster Museums pamphlet, 1982), pp. 17–18.
22. A. V. John, *By the Sweat of their Brow: Women workers in Victorian Coal Mines* (Croom Helm, 1980), p. 55.
23. *Report of the Commissioner on Mining Districts*, PP, 1846, xxiv, pp. 441–4.
24. Quoted in P. Horn, *The Victorian and Edwardian Schoolchild* (Stroud, Alan Sutton, 1989), p. 50.
25. Penn, *Manchester Fourteen Miles*, p. 203.
26. H. MacLeod in G. Crossick (ed.), *The Lower Middle Class in Britain 1870–1914* (Croom Helm, 1977), p. 63.
27. E. Higgs, 'Domestic Servants and Households in Victorian England', *Social History*, 8 (1983), p. 208.
28. Willoughby, 'Domestic Service', p. 36.
29. A. Adburgham, *Shops and Shopping 1800–1914* (1964, repr. Barrie and Jenkins, 1989), pp. 194–5.
30. Liddington and Norris, *One Hand Tied Behind Us*, p. 36.
31. *Report by Miss Collet on the Statistics of Employment of Women and Girls*, PP, 1894, lxxxi, Part II, pp. 863–8.
32. F. J. Marquis, *Handbook of Employments in Liverpool* (Liverpool Education Committee, 1916), p. 87.
33. J. Burnett, *Useful Toil: Autobiographies of Working People from the 1820s to the 1920s* (Allan Lane, 1974), pp. 221–2.
34. J. K. Walton, *The Blackpool Landlady: a Social History* (Manchester University Press, 1978), p. 134.
35. *Annual Report of the Board of Education 1905–6*, PP, 1906, xxviii, p. 177.
36. St Johns C.E. School Blackpool log book, 23 September 1867, LRO, SMBP 9/1.
37. Poulton Road Girls' School Morecambe, log book, June 1891, LRO, SMMC1/2
38. ibid., 2 October 1896.
39. *Employment of School Children*, PP, 1902, xxv, oral evidence of W. Bainbridge (QQ. 8996–9082) and written correspondence, p. 586.
40. Marquis, *Handbook of Employments*, p. 171.
41. Davies, *North Country Bred*, p. 61.
42. Oral History Collection CNWRS, Lancaster University, Respondent Mrs G.1.B.

43. Penn, *Manchester Fourteen Miles*, p. 214.
44. Roberts, *A Woman's Place*, p. 66.
45. Kirkby in Furness Co-operative Society Minutes, 1904, Barrow Record Office, BD8/22.
46. *Handbook of Employments*, p. 184.
47. *Return on Elementary Schools (Children Working for Wages) Part 2*, PP, 1899, lxxv, p. 576.
48. *Census of Great Britain*, County of Lancaster, Table 32. The percentage dropped to 56 for teachers over 35 years old.
49. L. Holcombe, *Victorian Ladies at Work* (David & Charles, 1973), p. 36.
50. Quoted in R. Gittings and J. Manton, *The Second Mrs Hardy* (Heinemann, 1979), p. 15.
51. F. Widdowson, '"Educating Teacher": Women and Elementary Teaching in London, 1900–1914' in L. Davidoff and B. Westover (eds.), *Our Work, Our Words, Our Lives: Women's History and Women's Work* (Macmillan, 1986), p. 122.
52. Wesleyan Day School, Blackpool log book, 9 September 1887, LRO, SMBP4/1.
53. Poulton Road Girls' School, Morecambe, log book 25 September 1878, LRO, SMMC 1/1.
54. The salaries of monitors and pupil-teachers as set by the Committee of Council on Education 1846 were

|  | Pupil-Teachers | | | Monitors | | |
|---|---|---|---|---|---|---|
| end of: | £ | s. | d. | £ | s. | d. |
| 1st year | 10 | 0 | 0 | 5 | 0 | 0 |
| 2nd year | 12 | 10 | 0 | 7 | 10 | 0 |
| 3rd year | 15 | 0 | 0 | 10 | 0 | 0 |
| 4th year | 17 | 0 | 0 | 12 | 0 | 0 |
| 5th year | 20 | 0 | 0 | | | |

55. C. McPhee and A. Fitzgerald (eds.), *The Non-violent Militant: Selected Writings of Teresa Billington Greig* (Routledge and Kegan Paul, 1987) p. 41.
56. Pulton Road Girls' School, morecambe, log book 29 October 1880, LRO, SMMC1/1.
57. Penn, *Manchester Fourteen Miles*, p. 125.
58. Wesleyan Day School, Blackpool, log book, 6 December 1889, LRO, SMB4/1.

# Afterthought: the past and the present

Michael Winstanley

*I see the Past, Present and Future existing all at once before me.*
*(William Blake)*

ANXIETY and apprehension about a perceived 'erosion of childhood' and a 'crisis of adolescence' characterise current debates about the young in Britain. There is widespread concern about low or deteriorating educational standards; a failure to provide sufficient relevant 'training' for future careers; work for adolescents which is unsuitable, seasonal, irregular, or casual; the breakdown of family relationships; a decline in moral values and a lack of respect for authority; the existence of street crime and child prostitution; the unhealthy influence of consumerism, the media and new forms of entertainment on the younger generation. Many of these problems are perceived to be of recent origin, the consequences of a period of unprecedented, rapid economic and social change. There was, it seems, an uncomplicated golden age not so long ago when children *were* children, families were united and happy, and moral standards were universally adhered to.

Historians are sceptical of idealised views of the past. It is not surprising, therefore, to find that many argue that our modern concept of 'childhood' is, to all intents and purposes, a recent construction and not one which would have been recognised by previous generations. The defining and redefining of the term is a continuing and complex process but, in the

138

words of Hugh Cunningham, 'Between the late seventeenth and mid-twentieth centuries there occurred a major and irreversible change in the representation of childhood, to the point where all children throughout the world were thought to be entitled to certain common elements and rights of childhood'.[1] In Britain the process was reflected in and determined by state legislation which defined and protected the rights of the young and moulded their experiences. This has prevented the exploitation of very young children in the labour market, introduced the principle of compulsory education and extended it to encompass all children up to the age of sixteen, and created extensive social welfare provisions designed to prevent abuse while promoting physical and emotional well-being.

This process was already evident in the last century and was heavily influenced by the increasing expressions of concern which were voiced about the perceived problems of child labour. Evidence of the widespread employment of young children which these debates generated should be sufficient to dispel many of the mythical, romantic, images of the innocence of 'childhood' during the period. Physically, working-class children may have matured more slowly a century ago, but in other respects they 'grew up' more quickly since the expectation was that they would be obliged to take on responsibilities or contribute to their upkeep at a much earlier age. The age at which children began work varied and not all the jobs they did aroused controversy, but clearly their experiences were far removed from the modern, idealised conception of what childhood is, or should be.

What is also striking about the debates on child labour is that, although the material realities of life were very different, the fears expressed about morality, education, training, welfare and the general upbringing of children were virtually identical to those of today. Then, as now, the concerns largely reflected the displaced fears and anxieties of adults, themselves struggling to come to terms with the implications of profound change. Then, as now, it was the literate, articulate members of society, the 'chattering classes' and professionals, who were the 'public' who voiced the most apprehension about the problems and who claimed to offer solutions. Then, as now, males were the main, although not the exclusive, focus of attention.

The agenda of vocal and literate campaigners inevitably tend to colour our perceptions of the past as well as the present. It is difficult to gauge the extent to which their expressions of concern, amounting in some cases to moral panics, were and are justified, or even whether they represent the views of the population as a whole; the voices of the majority of parents and children remain largely unheard. Debates which focus primarily on problems, however, invariably paint a partial picture of experience. Just as television documentaries and newspaper articles today do not deal with aspects of society which are not considered to be problematical, so official government enquiries and the polemical books and· pamphlets of the previous century, on which we are forced to rely for much of our understanding of the period, were written to point out problems and suggest reforms. This means that much of what happened, and what the bulk of the population thought of it, will remain forever hidden or difficult to piece together from the incomplete sources we have been left. All this makes it difficult to construct a rounded, impartial picture of the past or, indeed, the present.

This book has tried to show that children's experiences in Lancashire varied enormously depending on their social class, gender and whether they grew up in rural districts, textile districts, manufacturing towns, seaside resorts or commercial cities. Its primary intention has been to document this diversity and to explain why some, but not all, of the jobs which children did generated concern. Whether the differences in experience are still as marked today, whether the twentieth century has witnessed the 'erosion' or the 'creation' of childhood, and whether legislation has dictated or reflected public opinion, are complex questions to which this book cannot pretend to offer answers. Hopefully, however, it will have encouraged readers to question assumptions they might have had about children's experiences, present as well as past, and inspired some of them to find out more.

## Reference

1.  H. Cunningham, *The Children of the Poor: Representations of Childhood since the Seventeenth Century* (Blackwell, 1991), p. 7.

# Further reading and ideas for research

## Further reading

Apart from studies of education, the history of children has been relatively neglected by historians until comparatively recently. Since the 1970s, however, a number of important publications have appeared. This guide cannot list them all so it concentrates on those which should be reasonably easy to obtain and which are particularly relevant to the subject matter of this book; readers who wish to dig deeper should look at the sources listed in the footnotes and bibliographies in the following works. Most books should be obtainable at all good libraries, either directly or through inter-library loans; journals are probably only available in university and college libraries.

E. Hopkins, *Childhood Transformed: Working-Class Children in Nineteenth-Century England* (Manchester University Press, 1994) appeared after the research for this book was completed; it offers a readable overview of published literature which is more comprehensive than J. Walvin, *A Child's World: A Social History of English Childhood, 1800–1914* (Penguin, 1982). P. Horn, *The Victorian and Edwardian Schoolchild* (Stroud, Alan Sutton, 1989) is an attractively priced, illustrated survey, as is her earlier work, *The Victorian Country Child* (1974, repr. Alan Sutton, 1990) although the latter contains little Lancashire information. As its title implies, L. Rose, *The Erosion of Childhood: Child Oppression in Britain, 1860–1918* (Routledge, 1991) has strong views on the subject. For those wishing to delve deeper into the concept of childhood, H. Cunningham, *The Children of the Poor: Representations of Childhood since the Seventeenth Century* (Blackwell, 1991) provides much food for thought; as does his article in *Past and Present*, 126 (1990), 'The Employment and Unemployment of Children in England, c. 1680–1851'. J. H. Plumb, 'The New World of Children in Eighteenth-Century England',

*Past and Present*, 67 (1975), reprinted in N. McKendrick, J. Brewer and J. H. Plumb, *The Birth of a Consumer Society: the Commercialisation of Eighteenth-Century England* (Hutchinson pbk., 1983) deals with the growth of the market for children's products. A. Davin, 'Child Labour, the Working-Class Family, and the Domestic Ideology in 19th Century Britain', *Development and Change* 13 (1982) and H. Hendrick, 'The History of Childhood and Youth', *Social History*, 9 (1984) are very useful interpretative essays. H. Hendrick, *Child Welfare: England, 1872–1989* (Routledge, 1994) is a comprehensive history of social policy.

The history of male adolescents has received a lot of attention since the 1980s. First on the scene were S. Humphries, *Hooligans or Rebels? An Oral History of Working-Class Childhood and Youth, 1889–1939* (Blackwell, 1981), G. Pearson's highly readable *Hooligan: a History of Respectable Fears* (Macmillan, 1983) and J. Springhall, *Coming of Age: Adolescence in Britain* (Dublin: Gill & Macmillan, 1986). More recently two books specifically on the turn of the century have appeared: H. Hendrick, *Images of Youth: Age, Class and the Male Youth Problem, 1880–1920* (Clarendon Press, 1990) and M. J. Childs, *Labour's Apprentices: Working-Class Lads in Late Victorian and Edwardian England* (Hambledon Press, 1992). C. Dyhouse, *Girls Growing Up in Late Victorian and Edwardian England* (Routledge & Kegan Paul, 1981) is a useful discussion of the social constraints and values which dictated experience.

Not surprisingly, discussions of Lancashire children have focused on cotton and to a lesser extent, coal; there is nothing, to my knowledge, on children's work elsewhere in the county. Most books on the textile industry refer to child labour, especially in the early nineteenth century, but P. Bolin-Hart, *Work, Family and the State: Child Labour and the Organisation of Production in the British Cotton Industry, 1780–1920* (Lund University Press, Sweden, 1989), is the only comprehensive treatment of the subject. As its title implies, M. Cruickshank, *Children and Industry: Child Health and Welfare in North-West Textile Towns during the Nineteenth Century* (Manchester University Press, 1981) is mainly concerned with the consequences of urban life; C. Nardinelli, *Child Labor and the Industrial Revolution* (Indiana University Press, 1990) claims to be a radically new interpretation, but has received some critical reviews. E. and R. Frow, *A Survey of the Half-time System in Education* (Manchester, E. J. Morten, 1970) concentrates on the schooling aspects, as does H. Silver, 'Ideology and the Factory Child: Attitudes to

Half-time Education', in P. McCann (ed.), *Popular Education and Socialization in the Nineteenth Century* (Methuen, 1977). Lancashire Museums Education Service, *Children at Work* (compiled by Rachel Hasted, n.d.) is a model of its kind packed with information for teachers, as is the well-illustrated, essentially oral-based F. Millett, *Childhood in Oldham, 1890–1920* (Oldham Leisure Services, 1989). It is difficult to beat some of the older straightforward, if detailed, histories of the legislation affecting child labour: B. L. Hutchins and A. Harrison, *A History of Factory Legislation* (P.S. King, 1911), A. H. Robson, *The Education of Children Engaged in Industry in England, 1833–1876* (Kegan Paul, 1931), and M. W. Thomas, *The Early Factory Legislation* (1958).

## Ideas and sources for research

There is still plenty of scope for research into this subject at local level. Many of the sources are available in the county in university and local libraries, study centres, sound archives and the record offices in Manchester, Liverpool and Preston. A guide to all the places holding historical records is T. Wyke, *Directory of Local Studies in North West England* (1993, obtainable from Bibliography of North West England, Manchester Central Library, St Peter's Square, Manchester). This should be available for consultation in all reference libraries in the North West. Probably the best guide to specific sources are the footnotes and references in books and articles; for that reason we have listed the sources which we have used at the end of the chapters in this publication. Ideas for lines of enquiry can be culled from the publications listed above: the list is virtually endless; the development of schooling; patterns of and attitudes to work; health; family upbringing; welfare; games.

We still know surprisingly little as yet about the sorts of families which working children came from – the age of the parents, number of children, where they lived, etc. The published census returns after 1851 (especially in 1911) provide statistical tables but only for counties and large towns. The enumerators' original manuscript books allow a much more detailed picture of family and work in a specific district to be compiled and they are now available for 1841–1891 and can be consulted in local libraries.

Parliamentary Papers contain a wealth of material on an enormous range of subjects: reports; oral evidence; written submissions; statistical tables. You will find many of the more important ones referenced in the chapters in this book but only a fraction of what they contain has been included and there are many, many others. Some enquiries contain detailed descriptions of the type of work which children did. There are published guides to the contents of Parliamentary Papers and most of the publications have an index or detailed contents pages; even so, the sheer volume of material can be intimidating and it is not always easy to find local information. Some bound volumes of Royal Commissions' reports and evidence which have Lancashire material in them (e.g. 1833 Factory Commission; 1868 Schools Inquiry Commission) can be consulted at Lancashire Record Office [LRO] and Lancashire County Library Head-quarters [LCL HQ] (the latter by appointment only), but the majority are on microfiche or microcard in university and college libraries and it is advisable to seek assistance before using them.

Much of the published literature on the factory question of the early nineteenth century and turn-of-the-century 'boy labour' problem has been reprinted in recent years and is relatively easy to obtain. It contains a lot of information about specific parts of Lancashire but should be treated with caution since much of it was polemical. Local newspapers often contain details of prosecutions brought under the Factory Acts but are likely to prove time-consuming to use; *The Cotton Factory Times* is the best guide to developments in this industry and would repay detailed examin-ation. It can be consulted at LCL HQ, again by appointment only, and at Manchester Metropolitan University. Annual reports by Chief Con-stables and Schools Inspectors often contain information, as do printed local bye-laws, but school log books from the late nineteenth century are perhaps the most enjoyable and profitable way in for local studies: many are still held by the schools, but a significant number are now in the record offices.

The most accessible sources for the twentieth century are people's own recollections. Elizabeth Roberts's collection of interviews in Barrow, Lan-caster and Preston go back to the 1890s and can be consulted (by appoint-ment) at the Centre for North West Regional Studies, Lancaster University, or in the University Library. The North West Sound Archive at Clitheroe (with a listening post in LRO) is also an increasingly valuable asset, as is the Ambleside oral history collection. There is also an extensive oral history, photographic and film archive at Manchester Metropolitan University. But there is plenty of scope for carrying out one's own interviews: everyone has been a child and has recollections of school and of beginning work.